Daniel J. Cherico

To Bill and Lillian,
with our best wishes
tucked inside.
Joe & Sandy Bess

ENTHUSIASM AND DIVINE MADNESS

JOSEF PIEPER

ENTHUSIASM *and*
DIVINE MADNESS

On the Platonic dialogue PHAEDRUS
Translated from the German
by Richard and Clara Winston
A Helen and Kurt Wolff Book
Harcourt, Brace & World, Inc.
New York

The Author and the Translators
dedicate this book to the memory of
K U R T   W O L F F

Contents

IV

*The Kierkegaardian Reversal: evocation of the aesthetic
leads to religious truth.   The power of recantation and
repentance.   "Love among free men."   The emergence
of the images of the gods.   The masquerade goes
on.*   37

V

Mania *as a divine gift.   Madness, loss of autonomous
self-possession,* passio, *enthusiasm. Forms of "divine madness."   First: prophetic ecstasy: Delphi, Dodona, the
Sibyl.   Sterility of the historical point of view.   Enthusiasm, the key word.   How does revelation take place?
Second: "cathartic" mania.   Madness as precondition for
purification and healing.   Frenzy, poetry, and inspiration.   Lessing, Hölderlin, Goethe, Benn.   Who is "the
poet"?*   47

VI

*True possession of life can be had only by being "out of
one's wits."   The fourth form of* theia mania: *erotic emotion.   Nature and destiny of the soul.   Immortality.
Acquiring wings.   "Permeating the whole cosmos."
Figurative language as a manifestation of intellectual humility.   Parable and myth.   The fall of the soul.
Yearning and recollection.   Supremely beloved and supremely troubling: beauty.   "Beauty is not so much performance as promise" (Goethe).   The erotic nature of
philosophizing.   Forms and deformities of Eros.*   69

VII

VIII

Foreword

If we should ask historians of philosophy to name the four or five most important works of Plato, the answers will by no means be unanimous. That is natural enough. But the *Phaedrus* is fairly certain to be in their lists, along with the *Symposium*, the *Politeia*,* and the *Phaedo*.

The *Phaedrus* has had a curious fate in the Platonic scholarship of the past hundred years. According to one historian of philosophy, this dialogue was "up to very recently the hotly disputed center of Platonic scholarship." [1] The immediate cause of this dispute—namely, the question of the dialogue's date—will not concern us in the following pages. But the question itself has been kindled by the content and the form of the work. Moreover, the dispute involves a difference of far more than a few years or a decade. Some critics, for example Schleiermacher and Usener, have maintained that the *Phaedrus* is a very early work, perhaps the first book Plato wrote in his youth; while others say that the dialogue is obviously the product of age, that the philosopher must have been at least sixty when he wrote it—after having already written the

---

* I prefer to use the Greek name instead of the more familiar but misleading *Republic*.

Politeia and the *Symposium*. Kurt Hildebrandt states: "Had its authenticity not been too securely established by tradition, it would have been easy to prove its inauthenticity by the methods of historical criticism, in line with the mood of our supercritical age." [2]

In point of fact, the methods of historical criticism have by now fairly well proved that the *Phaedrus* is actually the work of Plato's maturity, written during that great decade to which the *Symposium*, the *Politeia*, and the *Phaedo* also belong.

I merely mention all this, but do not mean to go into the matter any further. Let us be grateful for the testimonial to the dialogue's historical authenticity, and for its attribution to the years of Plato's highest achievements. But now let us turn our attention exclusively to the content of the *Phaedrus*; let us examine what it says.

To be sure, as I have stated, the very peculiarity of what it says has led to such contradictory datings. Even in antiquity commentators were troubled by the diction and structure of the *Phaedrus*. We know that Hermeias, the Alexandrian Neoplatonist who wrote a commentary on the dialogue, felt called upon to defend Plato against a variety of charges: immaturity, stylistic excess, crudeness of argumentation, and so on.[3] Moreover, it seems at first glance strange, not to say alarming, that such a variety of terms has been used in the attempt to define the content of the *Phaedrus*. After all, it really should seem possible to say what the dialogue is all about. The various ancient subtitles—*On Beauty, On Love, On the Soul*—can in fact be reduced to a common denominator. Not so the statements of the theme which have been current since Schleiermacher's day, that is, since the beginning of the nineteenth century. Schleiermacher himself held that the real subject of the *Phaedrus* is "the art of untrammeled thinking and of creative communication, or *dialectics*." [4] Susemihl, likewise a translator of Plato and an important historian of philosophy, declared about 1850: "Anamnesis is the unifying point." [5] In 1898 the philosopher Paul Natorp stated in a treatise entitled *Plato's Phaedrus:* "The unifying idea is that of community." [6] Wilamowitz, in his influential book on Plato's life and work which was published immediately after the First World War, devoted a lengthy chapter to the *Phaedrus* in which the theme is defined in entirely different terms. "The mood induced by nature," he writes, "gave Plato the strength in a happy moment to sum up everything" in this dialogue. "Therefore I call this chapter, which treats of the *Phaedrus*, a felicitous summer day." And he adds fiercely: "People will scold or laugh at this; I know how it is. No matter: this is the way I see the poet whose soul I am trying to penetrate by empathy." [7]

I have saved the most astounding interpretation of the dialogue's theme for last. "The *Phaedrus*," the newest theory runs, "may well be venerated as the Holy Scriptures of the foundation of the 'Reich.'" This is put forth by Kurt Hildebrandt in the 1953 German edition of *Phaedrus*.[8]

All these divergent interpretations may make us consider thrice before we rush in with our own analysis of the *Phaedrus*. And I confess that I myself have hesitated for nearly ten years. On the one hand I have repeatedly been fascinated by certain passages in this dialogue. Its effect upon the best minds of the ages has been extraordinary—nor is it difficult to see why. Hölderlin, for example, wanted his own magnificent aesthetic doctrine to be understood as a kind of commentary on the *Phaedrus*. On the other hand, one is bewildered by the strange assortment of interpretations. From abstract didacticism to sentimental romanticism, elucidation has run wild. And the dialogue itself, as a literary work, is also a somewhat baffling matter at first and unfortunately at second glance. It seems to fall into two major parts which are quite distinct from each other. Moreover, they seem to have nothing whatsoever to do with each other.

This very "disproportion," Usener says, this awkward arrangement of the dialogue, is "a sure indication of the author's youth." [9] But if we consider only the first part, which is the most important, it turns out that it is fairly consistent thematically. On the other hand, this theme is discussed in an extremely strange manner. There are three speeches. The first of them is a quotation from beginning to end. Some interpreters believe it is meant as a parody of the supposedly quoted author. In any case, this first speech is presented as the statement of a man who is not present; it is read aloud. The second speech is delivered by Socrates himself; but almost as soon as he finishes it, he says that he did not mean any of it seriously, that it is all shamefully false. And then, in the third speech, he makes a detailed presentation of the exact opposite of what he had said before.

To fill the cup of confusion to the brim, moreover, scholars tell us that none of these three speeches, which take up a good half of the entire dialogue, means anything at all in terms of content; that they are rather mere samples, rhetorical models and practice pieces. Then does it mean nothing, we are bound to ask, that all three speeches deal with Eros? To which question we receive the answer that this subject possessed "a special attractiveness to the young men of Athens." [10]

Nevertheless, I believe it is worth attempting an interpretation of the *Phaedrus*. Those sections of it whose meanings can be deciphered with some certainty reveal, answer, illuminate so much of our human reality that we cannot but feel the dialogue is worth our close attention and our thought. Indeed, taken as a whole, it is always worth while—or perhaps I should say that it always behooves us—to listen to Plato. Not only in order to learn something about Plato, although we wish to do that too; but above all to become aware of certain fundamental aspects of existence which Plato sees, names, and tries to analyze. For we still stand before these aspects of existence in perplexity; we still need the interpretation.

In the following pages I do not claim to have found a "solution." Rather, we shall simply have to leave a good many enigmas as insoluble as ever. Nor will we be primarily concerned with looking for a single underlying idea. We shall also not look for a formula that might summarize the entire content of the dialogue in the manner of a headline. Nor shall we examine the question which has so long occupied the scholars, namely, how the *Phaedrus* fits into Plato's "philosophical system"; "the position in the system" is the title of one chapter in a work entitled *Structure and Character of Plato's Phaedrus*.[11] The fact is that there is no such thing as a Platonic system. Those who truly know Plato have time and again had to admit this. Plato, Wilamowitz tells us in his book, "actually arrived at no completely logical unity in his teachings and beliefs concerning the human soul." [12] This is quite true—but Wilamowitz continues the sentence in a highly questionable manner. Those who love Plato as a human being, he goes on, ultimately come around to "delighting in these very contradictions which are so intimately related to the man and to his soul."

I must confess that such a point of view strikes me as most disconcerting. And I try to imagine how Plato, or even Socrates, would have reacted if anyone had said to him: "To be sure, I see no logical connection in what you are saying, but I am glad that you are so vital a personality, so full of contradictions!" Rather, it seems to me, the value of Platonic insights stems from their having been gained from a close examination of the subject matter under discussion, from their having arisen straight out of the actual dialogue—*without* any thought of whether the result coordinates with other insights derived from elsewhere. Thus, the absence of a coherent system is not a sign of internal contradictions in Plato's mind, but—as is the case with other great thinkers, such as Aristotle, Augustine, and Thomas Aquinas—a mark of tacit respect for the unfathomability of the universe.

ENTHUSIASM AND DIVINE MADNESS

I

The "cast of characters." Components in the atmosphere of intellectual Athens: sophisticated detachment, enlightened "techniques for living," crude sensuality. Sophistry: "cultivated rationalization" (Hegel). Pseudo-wisdom and false contemporaneity. Success as a criterion. The "modernity" of Socrates: his concern is man, not nature. Mythical tales and myth as such.

The first line of the dialogue names the "cast of characters," the *dramatis personae*. We must not merely glance at this first line and pass on, for Plato's habit is to speak through the living personalities of the participants in his dialogues. Indeed, these characters themselves express his ideas almost more insistently than his theses and propositions.

The first line contains only two names: Socrates and Phaedrus.

The Socrates of this dialogue embodies seemingly irreconcilable features: wit, pleasure in mockery, and an inclination toward parody, such as we scarcely encounter in the other dialogues. But then we find the same man abruptly speaking in mythic images about the fate of the human soul. In elevated language he praises god-inspired escape from oneself in ecstasy. With the bold hand of a physician he uncovers the most intimate secrets of Eros.

And then he closes the discussion with a prayer. All in all, he strikes one, as Wilamowitz [1] says, as an altogether un-Socratic Socrates.

His interlocutor, Phaedrus, must have been an equally vivid character to the contemporary Athenian. And those of us today who want to hear the overtones, which Plato intended us to hear, must try as far as possible to reconstruct this vividness. We cannot stress too strongly the significance a Platonic dialogue must have had for the contemporary reader simply on the basis of its list of "participants." To our sensibility, Plato sometimes came perilously close to being almost unbearably direct. That becomes evident as soon as we attempt to translate Plato's way of going about things—in the *Symposium,* say—into the terms of our own time. It would be as though we overheard Albert Einstein, Ortega y Gasset, Bert Brecht, and Jean Cocteau in an imaginary conversation—imaginary and yet in subtle fashion extremely "real."

But, then, who is Phaedrus? He is one of the "learners" in Socrates' entourage, one of those young Athenians who are enthusiastically and uncritically devoted to their master, but who also tend to be lured by all the latest sensational fads.

Plato sketches these young men with undisguised irony. He lays bare their immaturity, their seductibility, their excessiveness. But his irony is affectionate; it strikes the note of a grown man contemplating his own youth. And it may really be, it seems to me, that Plato (who as we know is persistently silent about himself in the dialogues) may in fact have portrayed himself in these young Athenians. At any rate, we would probably be grasping only half of Plato's intention if we simply characterized Phaedrus as

4

an "uncritical culture vulture"[2] or a person of callow enthusiasms and superficial education who easily falls victim to any kind of speciousness.[3] Of course this latter characterization is true; Plato himself says the same thing. But Plato also tells us more—for example, that Phaedrus delivers one of the finest of the speeches of the *Symposium* in praise of love. (In similar fashion Plato dignifies Apollodorus, whom the Athenians took to calling "the madman" after he became a follower of Socrates, by making him the reporter of what went on during the feast in Agathon's house.)

In the present dialogue Phaedrus is Socrates' sole interlocutor. But he emerges from a group of characters who were equally well known to the reader of Plato's day, and some of whom were distinctly unsavory. Phaedrus must have poked his nose deep into that atmosphere spiced by so many and various essences. The first lines of the dialogue read as follows: "*Socrates*. Where do you come from, Phaedrus my friend, and where are you going? *Phaedrus*. I've been with Lysias, Socrates, the son of Cephalus, and I'm off for a walk outside the wall, after a long morning's sitting there. On the instructions of our common friend Acumenus I take my walks on the open roads; he tells me that is more invigorating than walking in the colonnades. *Socrates*. Yes, he's right in saying so. But Lysias, I take it, is in town. *Phaedrus*. Yes, staying with Epicrates, in that house where Morychus used to live, close to the temple of Olympian Zeus."

We may be inclined to regard this as a mere introduction to the real subject matter of the dialogue, and a rather lame and unoriginal introduction at that. In actuality it is already part and parcel of the real subject. But this becomes apparent only if we know the personalities concealed behind those names which are dropped so carelessly, without further explanation.

The first of them, Lysias, is a Sophistic speech-writer, a literary man of great technical ability, master of a distinguished prose style. His persuasiveness when he is lying is especially admirable.[4] Phaedrus in a moment will call him "the ablest writer of our day." Moreover, he is the scion of a respected conservative family; but this "younger generation" has broken with its fathers in revolutionary fashion. The upheavals of the last years of the Peloponnesian War—which came close to being a Thirty Years' War—are destroying the old order of things. When the war ends, Lysias is expropriated, his brother executed, and he himself goes into exile. The first speech he writes is an indictment of his brother's murderer. Here, then, is a biography which might very well have been cast in a "heroic" mode.

At the beginning of the great dialogue on the State, Socrates finds Lysias' father, Cephalus, sitting in the inner court of his home, wearing a garland, for he had been sacrificing. Socrates asks him what seems to him to have been the greatest blessing of his life; and the old man begins to tell about his cares: he wonders whether the traditional stories of reward and punishment after death may not be true after all; and so he is trying to draw up his reckoning with himself and to restore any unjustly acquired goods (330 d)—and so on.

Another sector of this enlightened society is made up of the devotees of the "better technique for living" cult, the health faddists and subscribers to the modish "back to nature" movement which, it must be said, is both anxiously followed and at the same time sneered at by this very society. Typical examples of these highly fashionable health reformers are Acumenus and his son Eryximachus, who incidentally is Phaedrus' particular friend, or more precisely, his lover. This is the same Eryximachus who at the beginning of the *Symposium* is barely stopped from delivering a technical medical speech on the evil effects of drunkenness.

Epicrates, with whom Lysias is staying, is characterized by Aristophanes as a "rhetorician and demagogue." He is, it seems, a rather doubtful customer who is somewhat cavalier about the distinction between Mine and Thine. Ultimately he will be condemned to death for treason and bribery.[5] As for Morychus, I shall merely quote the terse note given in Pauly-Wissowa: "Tragedian, undoubtedly of the lowest rank, whose principal interests were culinary pleasures." [6]

Thus, in the first lines of the dialogue, Plato evokes the atmosphere in which these young Athenian intellectuals live. Theirs is a world of sophisticated irreverence and detachment, of enlightened health doctrines and simultaneous depravity. And in the midst of these poisonous fumes, strangely untouched but gravely imperiled, we find Phaedrus! Coming straight from such company, he meets Socrates, who at once asks him what his friends had talked about. Though he already can surmise: No doubt Lysias gave the company a feast of eloquence, served up his latest, just completed "show pieces."

It turns out that this guess is correct. Moreover, this time, Phaedrus says, the subject was something which especially concerns Socrates: "The topic is appropriate for your ears, Socrates." For Lysias' new literary work is a *logos erotikos,* a speech about love. The "ablest writer of our day," Phaedrus says, has brought to light something incredibly subtle, entirely new and original, on this age-old and inexhaustible theme. As in almost all the Platonic dialogues, the situation in the *Phaedrus* is from the start governed by the enthusiasm of the younger generation for Sophistry. Perhaps we should term it fascination and enchantment rather than enthusiasm. Plato himself in the dialogue *Protagoras* (310 f) has depicted what must remain the classical example of this attitude. He describes in detail how Hippocrates, who is very young, comes running long before dawn to Socrates, and wakes him. Socrates anxiously asks whether anything bad has happened. Whereupon Hippocrates thinks no further explanation is needed than the announcement that Protagoras has arrived. He insists that Socrates must introduce him to the famous Sophist, at once! The young man is ready to sacrifice all his money, and if necessary his friends' money also.

Phaedrus is the same type as Hippocrates. If he could only say by heart all that this man has said, it would mean more to him "than coming into a fortune," he declares. And, of course, above all say it *the way* Lysias said it. Socrates pretends to be all agog at this. He insists that

Phaedrus tell him what Lysias said. "I won't leave you even if you extend your walk as far as Megara." By tempting him with the promise of hearing such speeches, he continues, Phaedrus could lead him all around Attica, the way a hungry goat is led by holding green leaves before it.

When Phaedrus becomes coy, Socrates grows impatient.

He chaffs Phaedrus by once more describing the boy's bemused state: Phaedrus must have been listening to Lysias' speech being repeated all morning until he grew weary and went for a walk, reciting the speech to himself. ("Upon my word, I believe he had learnt the whole speech by heart.") And then, to his great pleasure, out in the country he came upon the man "who has a passion for listening to discourses." He met, that is, "someone to share his frenzied enthusiasm." And he insists that Phaedrus drop his pretended reluctance and quote the speech, since he obviously can scarcely wait to do so.

228
d 6 As soon as Phaedrus begins, Socrates interrupts him again. "Show me what it is that you have in your left hand under your cloak; for I surmise that it is the actual discourse." And he insists that Phaedrus read it aloud.

This enthusiasm of Athenian youth for Sophistry may sometimes seem to us slightly improbable. But we must realize that it was a fact if we wish to understand not only Plato's tone, but also his concern, and the urgency of that concern.

We really should discuss Sophistry in somewhat greater detail; but of course that is not possible in this context. However, we shall permit ourselves three brief remarks.

First: The great Sophists were not just a group of peculiar intellectual harlequins who proclaimed abstruse ideas. Rather, they represented a level of intellectualism which had reached the ultimate degree of perfection possible at the time. The historians are right in speaking of them as founders of formal education in the West. Werner Jaeger calls the Sophists "the first humanists." [7] Hegel says that the Sophists embody "cultivated rationalization in general." [8] If we look for contemporary analogies to the phenomenon of Sophistry, we would have to search among the most advanced representatives of *haute littérature*.

Second: It is inherent in the nature of Sophistry that it is difficult to pin it down. Above all, the destructive element in it is hard to recognize. All his life Plato was constantly making new efforts to do so. In a dialogue written very late in life, entitled *The Sophist*, he went back to the very beginnings to ask: Just what is a Sophist? As is well known, so brilliant a man as Aristophanes regarded Socrates as a Sophist. In other words, Socrates was confounded with the extreme antithesis to his own nature. What this means is that Aristophanes did not understand the Sophists. Aristotle, for his part, repeatedly defined Sophistry as *pseudo*-wisdom. John Wild, the distinguished American interpreter of Plato, says: The Sophist "seems just like a philosopher. He talks just like a philosopher. In fact we may say that he appears even more like a philosopher than the philosopher himself." [9]

Third: Sophistry is a phenomenon which, as Hegel says, "recurs in all ages," [10] and which we must therefore be prepared to encounter in every epoch. It is inherent in the nature of Sophistry to expound the avant-garde ideas of any given time. It always presumes to be exactly what is necessary and correct "now"; to be the timely and modern thing. Sophistry and topicality are co-ordinate concepts in a highly specific sense. Of course this does not mean that avant-gardism is always and necessarily Sophistical; but in this realm we must constantly be prepared for masquerade. Sophistry is "pseudo-contemporaneity"—but the sham is difficult to unmask.

If we consider carefully what Plato said about the Sophists and how he represented them, we will realize that he evidently perceived exactly what was dangerous about them for *all* ages, and that he identified that dangerous element. There are a number of points in the teachings of the Sophists which are just as pertinent today as they were in fourth-century Athens. For example: after Socrates, accompanied by young Hippocrates, has made his way to Protagoras early in the morning, he asks the celebrated sage what one can learn from him. The answer runs: You can learn from me how to make your way successfully through life, as a private person and also as a citizen. Such competence in life is considered to be *areté*, virtue (*Protagoras*, 318 e). Thus, in the teachings of Protagoras, the measure of man is equated with his capacity to achieve success: rightness means success. But is this Sophistic conception of rightness so very remote from those views of man in which utility is made the standard for every human action and, to express this in less totalitarian terms, efficiency represents the supreme value? In both cases, be it noted, what is involved is not merely the factual and practical aspect of life, but a value-judgment and a program: Everything that serves success is good; everything that hinders it is bad. But what hinders success? Philosophical *theoria*, for example, that is to say, that mode of approaching the world which aims solely or chiefly at one single thing: to find out the nature of reality. Philosophical *theoria* aims at truth and nothing else. Cicero and Seneca translated the word *theoria* into Latin; and the word they chose to render it was *contemplatio*. We need only say the word to realize how contemporary the Sophistic thesis is. But it is not only contemplation—the *vita contemplativa* —that hinders the man who has made his principal goal to become "master and owner of nature" (to use Descartes's phrase [11]). He will also be hindered by the violent emotions which may make him forget the practical aims of

1 1

life; violent emotion in the face of death, for example, or from experiencing the superhuman; or, also, the violent emotion of love. The alternatives are avoidance of existential emotions by practicing a rational life pattern, by methodical exclusion of everything that cannot be planned (which includes both utilitarian social planning and individual programs for a "successful" life). Instead of genuine inner upheaval, artificial intoxicants and excitements can be administered in careful doses. And the reason that Sophism continues to have pertinence, across the span of ages, is that the theories and programs of Sophistry purvey these alternatives.

It is precisely this sort of thing that is the kernel of the speech by Lysias, a copy of which Phaedrus is carrying under his cloak and about which he is so enthusiastic. It is a speech about love, Eros. Phaedrus sums up its content in a single sentence: Lysias maintains that handsome boys should give their favor to non-lovers rather than to lovers. Therein, Phaedrus adds, lies the subtlety, the cleverness, the gist of this speech.

Now we may say: Is that not sheer nonsense, simply an arbitrary conceit, a silliness invented merely for the sake of being *outré*? But the matter is not so simple. Whatever the finer details of the argument, it is clear that the speech proposes as a normative standard desire and enjoyment *without love*.[12]

As we read along in the dialogue, no further explanation is offered. The statement is merely made and then, so it seems, completely forgotten for a while. Phaedrus seems to be impressed solely by the formal elegance of the language and structure of the speech, by the refinement in the use of antithesis, and the enormous stylistic talent

Lysias has displayed. The style seems to have claimed all his attention and admiration. The content is scarcely regarded. Probably a similar reaction may often be observed in the younger generation of any age. The young wax enthusiastic over the most destructive, most shocking, most immoral theories—and upon closer examination it turns out that they are almost entirely indifferent to the content of such statements. They are fascinated by the unusual, by the elegance and excessiveness of presentation.

Socrates does not immediately turn his attention to the content of the speech, either. His response is purely ironical; he comments that if favor were thus granted to a poor man rather than a rich one, or an old man rather than a young one, then at least it would benefit him, Socrates. All this is mere gay, sociable chatter, a long way from serious discourse.

227
c 9

Nevertheless, as a writer Plato does not go in for mere padding. While the two, Socrates and Phaedrus, saunter away from the city, walking along the brook Ilissus and finally wading barefoot in its waters, something definite "happens." The pair show us more plainly the kind of people they are. And Socrates shows us a wholly new side of himself. He stands before a tall plane tree and finds it all lovely: the fragrance, the gentle breeze, the water, the grass. But he speaks of it as though he were seeing all this for the first time. You strange man, Phaedrus says, you talk like a foreigner being shown the country by a guide. Don't you ever set foot outside the walls of the city? Whereupon Socrates makes a reply which does more than throw a sidelight on his own personality; it sums up a whole epoch of intellectual history. "Trees and open country," he says, "won't teach me anything, whereas men in

230
c 6

the town do." The philosophers whom we call the pre-Socratics inquired into the structure of the cosmos. This new generation, to which both the Sophists and Socrates belong, do not just give a new answer (to the old question); they ask different questions. What primarily interests them is no longer nature, the cosmos, but *man*.

Phaedrus asks another question, again quite incidentally. The two pass by a spot which reminds Phaedrus of the traditional story of the rape of the nymph Oreithyia by Boreas, and he asks whether it happened here, by the Ilissus. "But pray tell me, Socrates, do you believe that story to be true?"

229
c 4

To this Socrates replies in a somewhat enigmatic way. If I disbelieved this story, as the men of science do, I would not be at a loss; I would talk away cleverly and explain that the north wind blew the girl from a high cliff and people then said: She has been seized by Boreas. That sort of interpretation is always possible in a given case. But then what about Centaurs and Chimeras, Gorgons and Pegasuses? Obviously, not all such stories could be explained in the same manner. Anyone who attempted to do so would have to have a great deal of time at his disposal. Consequently, Socrates goes on, I don't bother about such things; I believe in them as custom demands. What really concerns me is the question of who I myself am: "I can't as yet 'know myself,' as the inscription at Delphi enjoins."

This reply has been taken to represent Socrates' view of the "myths," and has been interpreted as follows: He is indifferent to the myths; what interests him is the ethical subject's rational knowledge of self; he respects superrational information of mythic origin, but feels he has no time to dwell on it.

1 4

The matter is, as I have said, rather complicated and cannot be discussed in detail here. But I think the following point is the decisive one: There are mythic tales, and there is Myth as such; there are a variety of traditions, and there is Tradition. Myth and Tradition as such bear on the heart of existence; they bear on man's salvation. Wherever these concepts crop up in the Platonic writings —as, for example, in the narratives of the origin of the universe, of the primal state and fall of man, of judgment after death—Socrates clearly and strongly proclaims his unconditional veneration. On such occasions Socrates does not talk about having no time for Myth; he goes to considerable lengths to delve into its meaning.

II

Except for a single reference, so far nothing has been said of the subject of the dialogue: love. But we have been made cognizant of the situation in which the discourse will take place. One of the chief elements of that situation is the pervasive "postwar mood" of detachment. It is a rather snobbistic attitude and is characterized by a lack of ties or allegiances of any sort. From this standpoint, a respect for tradition indicates a lack of real quality; "the man of true intelligence tracks down defects." [1] The scarcely dissimulated sensuality is combined with a scientific interest in techniques for living. All this is articulated and made acceptable by means of the verbal magic of Sophistry. And the class of young intellectuals is fascinated, bewitched, hypnotized by it all. On the other hand, they are oddly innocent and immune to the really destructive aspects of such detachment because their enthusiasm is roused more by form than by content, more by manner than by matter. One of these boys, Phaedrus—he, too, simultaneously fascinated and immune, still ecstatic over Lysias' speech on love which he has just heard—meets Socrates, as we have seen. And Socrates is almost offensively sober, is an outspoken anti-Sophist. But at the same time he is passionately stirred by the same questions that excite the younger generation. Herein Socrates does not show the stuffy conservatism of the usual Athenian anti-Sophists. He is just as "modern" as the Sophists; he completely accepts the questions they raise; he shares their exclusive interest in man. His differences with them concern not the questions, but the answers. This, then, is the man with whom Phaedrus is walking. The two settle down under a plane tree by the Ilissus. "Proceed," Socrates says. Whereupon Phaedrus takes out the roll of manuscript. "Here you are then." And he reads Lysias' speech.

230
e 4

If we were approaching this dialogue of Plato's from a scholarly point of view, we would be brought up short once more at this point. A speech by Lysias? Are we really to believe that Plato quotes word for word many pages by another writer? Some Plato scholars, among them Wilamowitz, Friedländer, Hildebrandt, answer this question affirmatively. And their arguments are worth a hearing. First, the speech exactly corresponds to Lysias' style as we have met it elsewhere. Second, "It would be *impossible* for Plato arbitrarily to attribute to the famous orator [Lysias] a speech which he then dissects." [2] Third, to introduce this foreign element into the dialogue which acts "like the yeast in the dough" [3] is an immensely clever stylistic device. Other interpreters, for example Hackforth and Weinstock, maintain that of course Plato was enough of a writer to invent a speech precisely in the style of Lysias, that, indeed, he is prone to do so, as the speeches of Aristophanes and Agathon in the *Symposium* demonstrate. Each man is

18

given his own individual and unmistakable diction, down to the subtlest nuance—and no one has ever come forth with the absurd idea that at most a quarter of the *Symposium* is Plato's own work. Moreover, Hackforth points out,[4] Plato is not at all concerned with Lysias as an individual; he is interested, rather, in the entire school. ("Lysias or someone else"—the phrase is actually repeated several times in the *Phaedrus*.)

Once again I mention this controversy only to drop it. It seems to me there is no way of settling it with a conclusive argument. All that really interests us here is Plato's obvious opinion that such a speech is possible, in form and above all in content; possible for and probably characteristic of a man whom such bright young men as Phaedrus regard as the most important writer of the times.

Now what of the speech itself? Right at the beginning of his conversation with Socrates, Phaedrus gave a brief sketch of it: "The discussion . . . concerned love. Lysias, you must know, has described how a handsome boy was tempted, but not by a lover; that's the clever part of it; he maintains that surrender should be to one who is not in love rather than to one who is."

227
c 5

Kurt Hildebrandt says: "This speech is profoundly ambiguous, and one is tempted to see it as unequivocally *base*." But, he continues, that cannot be what is meant, for if it were "the meaning of the whole dialogue would be distorted." [5]

The matter is really exceedingly complicated. But before we attempt to analyze the content of the speech, it will be worth our while to glance once more at its formal structure. Lysias is, as we have said, a writer of speeches; he composes speeches which are delivered by someone else. It is therefore part of his trade to identify with the mind of another man and to put words into that man's mouth. In our present case the other man is someone who is suing for the favor of a handsome boy. The speech is therefore a courtship speech. On the other hand, it is also "fiction"; it is an *as-if* courtship speech. Moreover, it is a fragment; it begins at a point after the essence of the speech has already been stated. This essence, which would be the central feature of a real courtship, is assumed; it is passed over in silence, but in such a manner that no misunderstanding is possible: "You know how I am situated, and I have told you that I think it to our advantage that this should happen." With these words, which sound rather like a concluding sentence, the speech begins. Thus the literary artistry, the stylistic skill, is linked with something altogether different. What appears to be aristocratic discretion actually serves to conceal something altogether coarse. Friedländer calls it the partnership of physical gratification and gabble.[6] Here speaks a man who desires and admittedly does not love; and his speech serves to conceal and to efface the brutish instinctual drive that is bent only on crude enjoyment, "physical desire and nothing else."[7] On the other hand, this eloquence also attempts to justify the lack of real love, the non-involvement of the human person. What is really so bad, in fact inhuman, about this attitude is not the craving for sensual gratification, but the deliberate, systematic separation of sensuality from spirituality, of sex from love.

This separation is—if we now consider content—the real subject of the speech which Phaedrus reads aloud to Socrates: "Now I claim that I should not be refused what I ask simply because I am not your lover."

231
a 1

There are three things which are united here in the medium of artfully differentiated language. The first is a discreetly concealed aim which, however, is fully understood, is taken completely for granted, and is pressed with implacable consistency: sensual gratification in the most drastic meaning of the term. Or as A. E. Taylor puts it: "Utility in the most sordid sense of the word." [8] The second is an emphatic and explicit rejection and devaluation of erotic emotion, of the *passio amoris*. Here *passio* does not mean passion in the sense of excessive vehemence; rather, it means only that one is seized by a superior force, that one is carried away by something. Moreover, the whole self is carried away; the force is an overwhelming one, not merely an isolated stimulus; rather, one is affected as a physical and spiritual being. Lysias' argument explicitly rejects this passive aspect of love, passive in the sense of something happening to the self. Third: the almost technical objectivity of mere sensual gratification (a woman is "taken" as a glass of water is drunk to quench thirst) is presented as something ethically valuable, as prudence, good sense, "virtue." Lysias actually uses the word *areté* in contradistinction to *love* ("not as a lover, but by virtue . . ."). Against this the erotic emotion appears to be something antipathetic to orderliness, to be folly and irrationality, not to say sickness. With what sounds like moral indignation Lysias bids us only to look at the "lovers"; they themselves know they are sick and admit it. Even in the Biblical Song of Songs (2, 5; 5, 8), in one of the very few passages in which the word *amor* occurs at all in the Latin Vulgate, the phrase is *amore langueo*, "I am sick with love."

The Sophists, then, with their ideas on proper living

technique, deplore and repudiate such excess. And they do so, be it noted, not in the name of any ascetic ideal and ethical control of the will, but in the name of being "without illusions." But such "realism" is actually nothing but lack of capacity for devotion; it is egocentric fear that a pleasure may be lost; it is spiritual poverty and deprivation. Lysias' speech, with its vast apparatus of words, rhetoric, and argumentation, attempts to represent desire without love, craving for pleasure without the capacity for emotion, as something quite meaningful and desirable. We must realize this with utter clarity; otherwise we shall not understand the polar opposite which Plato then conjures up for us. That opposite is the portrait of a soul which receives into its depths the emotion aroused by sensuous beauty, and simultaneously renounces physical gratification of that beauty. We are tempted to say that this same conception is to be found in the works of Paul Claudel. But that would certainly be anticipating.

We must once more look at the speech which Phaedrus has read aloud to Socrates under the noonday shade of the plane tree by the Ilissus. The three factors we have mentioned (the tacit but unequivocal aim of sensual pleasure; the deprecation of *passio*; the elevation of incapacity for emotion and devotion to "prudence," "good sense," "virtue") constitute the sustaining idea, the true content of the speech. But the speechmaker is highly "cultivated," and he therefore, while expositing these basic ideas, cannot help introducing a good deal that is true and correct, or at least significant and highly suggestive. His talent in this direction makes the line of argument so much the harder to see through. For example, the orator is absolutely right when he says that the excess inherent in every passionate emotion makes a person inept in dealing with the practical affairs of life. Those happenings which cannot be predicted, which pierce the soul, which come as overwhelming, transforming emotional upheavals, can *in toto* hardly be fitted into the orderly system of a rational conduct of life. Yet on the other hand man by virtue of his nature is indeed called upon to conduct his life rationally. There is an everlasting problem involved here—a problem both for ethical theory and for practical conduct. The Stoic ideal of a life without passion ever and again commends itself by its plausibility. Nevertheless it must perforce lead to a perhaps respectable but at bottom unnatural stasis. It is in the nature of man as a physical and spiritual being that he be open to shattering emotion, susceptible to being carried away. The *passiones animae* cannot be silenced without leading to inhumanity, either the inhumanity of rigid rationality or of brutish sensuality—both of which have in common the qualities of being "unromantic," "objective," and "safe from emotion." Real man is a being by nature given to shattering emotion. A good deed is better for having been committed with passion. Of course it is also true that a bad deed committed with passion is all the worse.[9]

Of course Lysias is stating a truth, though a trivial one, in saying that only the lover knows jealousy, whereas the non-lover is free of that particular folly. How indeed could jealousy exist in the realm of mercenary "love"?

The following argument deserves more consideration: We also love our children, our mothers and fathers, after all—and yet this love is not passion, not shattering erotic emotion, not frenzy. Here we are approaching matters which are hard to put into words; we can only touch on them. First, we should consider the remarkable fact that language does not use the word "lover" for parents loving their children, nor for children loving their parents, nor for brothers and sisters loving one another, nor for those linked in friendship. And when the mystics seek an analogy for the love of God, they find their comparison in erotic love which is kindled by physical beauty; we must read once more Francis de Sales's explanation for his calling his famous book not *Traité de la dilection de Dieu*, but *Traité de l'amour de Dieu*.[10]

There are, then, a variety of clever, thought-provoking, and difficult arguments that Lysias, or whoever may be concealed behind his name, winds like garlands around the fundamentally slender scaffolding of his real thesis.

After reading the speech, Phaedrus exclaims again: Isn't that extraordinarily fine? How, Kurt Hildebrandt asks, can "the noble Phaedrus" read such a thing "without repugnance"? To Hildebrandt, this innocent enthusiasm seems to prove that the speech—however much Lysias would be capable of advocating "the cold baseness of enjoyment without love"—cannot really be meant so crudely as the language suggests.[11] Certainly all this is *not* in keeping with the character of young Phaedrus. His own speech on love, with which the *Symposium* begins, cannot be mentioned in the same breath with Lysias' speech. The *Symposium* shows us an enthusiastic Phaedrus stirred by the power of Eros; he does not say a word about the gratification of desire or even of the bliss of feeling. Instead, his speech concerns the uttermost that can be demanded of man, the *ultimum potentiae*, which the lover alone would be ashamed not to meet; only love makes man capable of vicarious sacrifice, indeed, of heroic acceptance of death.

Nobility, love of honor, bravery are the virtues which distinguish the lover—such is the style and tone of Phaedrus' speech in the *Symposium*. And this same Phaedrus regards Lysias' speech on the same theme of love as "extraordinarily fine"! We must, however, read the sentence to the end—"especially in point of language." Phaedrus, that is, is impressed particularly by the manner, the diction, the linguistic virtuosity. His enthusiasm is primarily kindled by the purely formal element. The content does not seem to interest him—which, of course, does not mean that the thesis may not take effect after all, perhaps imperceptibly. What is happening here is, as we have said, something extremely typical. The fascinating aspect of Sartre, Brecht, Ionesco is their *manner*; content and substance are not only beside the point, but to speak of them is to prove oneself a vulgarian. Are the works of these men true or false, good or bad, constructive or destructive, misleading, seductive?—such questions are asked only by those who do not understand great literature. Plato, then, would undoubtedly have to be reckoned among such vulgarians; for he banished Homer, whom he had loved and admired from his youth on, from his republic because the great poet related unworthy things about the gods.

But it is not enough for Phaedrus to admire the speech all by himself; he seeks confirmation from a fellow enthusiast. "What do you think of the speech, Socrates?" And Socrates complies with his wish: the speech is *daimonios*, "devilishly fine indeed. . . . I was thrilled by it!" When Socrates talks this way, we should of course be on our guard. Anyone who has the slightest familiarity with the Platonic dialogues knows the cunning ingenuity with which Socrates delights in playing the part of being wholly taken in, utterly enchanted by Sophistic verbal magic. His own Apology begins with such an admission: his accusers, he says, have spoken so persuasively that they have almost made him forget who he was. The strongest statement of this sort is probably to be found in the dialogue *Menexenus*, in which Socrates talks of the speeches which are customary at patriotic ceremonies honoring those who have died for their country, and in which every imaginable praise is lavished not only upon the dead but also upon the living, all of whom—insofar as they are Athenians—are glorified:

"I stand listening to their words, Menexenus, and become enchanted by them, and all of a sudden I imagine myself to have grown up into a greater and nobler and finer man than I was before. . . . This consciousness of dignity lasts me more than three days, and not until the fourth or fifth day do I come to my senses and know where I am. In the meantime I have been living in the Islands of the Blest, such is the art of our rhetoricians. . . ."

Therefore we must be on the alert. Socrates has said that he was thrilled. However, he goes on to say that he was especially delighted with the sight of Phaedrus' enthusiasm.

234
d 2 "I took my cue from you, and therefore joined in the ecstasy of my right worshipful companion."

This solemn and quite un-Socratic remark makes Phaedrus uneasy. "Come, come! Do you mean to make a joke of it?" He does not want to be dislodged from his ecstatic mood. "Tell me truly, as one friend to another, do you think there is anyone in Greece who could make a more important speech on the same subject?"

To this Socrates responds by asking a question in his turn: What do you mean by important? Are you referring to the content or the form? Do you mean the kind of thing

that must be judged from the point of view of truth or falsehood, or do you mean the manner? Socrates, it seems, is
not yet ready to enter into serious discussion of the subject,
and so he attempts to linger over the formal aspect, which
he really regards as unimportant. He goes on to say that
he has not considered the content, and after all knows nothing about such matters; all that interested him was the
rhetoric. And the rhetoric, he must add, was poor; the same
thing repeated three times, little inventiveness; perhaps
Lysias wanted to demonstrate that he could say the same
thing one way and then again in a different way, each time
with equal style!

But Phaedrus refuses to be put off. He considers his
hero's speech magnificent in both form and content; Lysias
has not overlooked any important aspect of the subject, and
no one could possibly have discussed it better.

Abruptly the seriousness of the conversation is restored,
although only briefly. Socrates says with great firmness:
235
b 7
"No!" If I were to admit you were right about this, I would
be confuted by the wise men and women of the past, the
Ancients, the *palaioi*; for they spoke differently about love.
And now, in spite of the gay and sociable lightness of tone
—perhaps we may say in spite of the almost drowsy idle-
ness of the talk—there follows a crucial statement about
the Ancients and his own relationship to them. Phaedrus
wants to know exactly whom Socrates is referring to. *Who*
are these Ancients? Who said anything better than Lysias?
235
c 2
Socrates' reply is deliberately vague: "I can't tell you off-
hand; but I'm sure I have heard something better, from
the fair Sappho maybe, or the wise Anacreon, or perhaps
some prose writer." At any rate, he continues, he has other
ideas about the matter, and certainly somewhat better ones.

235
d

He couldn't have hit upon these himself. "So I suppose it can only be that it has been poured into me, through my ears, as into a vessel, from some external source; though in my stupid fashion I have actually forgotten how, and from whom, I heard it."

We must, as has been said, imagine all this as spoken by Socrates with extreme nonchalance as he lies under the plane tree in the noonday heat; he is only half serious, and tosses in a high-sounding quotation from the poets ("There is something welling up within my breast"; this is simply high spirits, as we might toss off a tag from Shakespeare when we happened to be feeling good). Nevertheless, if I were asked to name a classical text which best expresses the mysterious and nevertheless unquestionable presence of the great and sacred tradition in the minds of the best pre-Christian thinkers, I would probably choose this passage. For what does it say? That the knowledge has come down from the "Ancients"; it is echoed in the poets; the vessel of the mind has been filled by hearing, that is to say, not out of personal experience and personal observation, but from external sources; yet the "how" and the "from whom" is forgotten.

235
c 5

Irony hampers interpretation. Socrates' first speech: unmasking by literal acceptance. The "daimonic" sign. The lightning bolt of forthright language.

Irony adds certain difficulties to conversation. If we are dealing with someone who is fond of speaking in ironic quotation marks, of pretending to be stupid while building up a powerful argument, of playing the enthusiast while practicing incisive criticism—then we must be infernally careful. We must keep our eyes and ears open, lest we miss some telltale shade of facial expression or intonation.

This is exactly how we must conduct ourselves toward Plato's Socrates. We must examine his face keenly; is he being serious now, or is he only making game of Phaedrus —and therefore of us as well? It is fairly easy to see through his exaggerated plaudits for Lysias' speech, which he promptly qualifies, although even that is in ironical terms. But now the conversation between Socrates and Phaedrus continues with Socrates answering the speech of Lysias by one of his own. After all, he had said that he could compose a different and better speech. And Phaedrus instantly held him to this: Very well, I offer a prize—a golden statue of you to be set up in the temple at Delphi, if you do as you say and make a better speech on the same

235
d 9

2 9

subject, no shorter and above all completely different, "which shall owe nothing to it."

Socrates tries another dodge; of course he did not mean it that way, it would obviously be impossible to make every detail new; even the poorest writer cannot help but make some good points. Phaedrus agrees in part; it will be all right for Socrates to retain the basic idea (that love is a sickness); but everything else must be new and original.

Socrates now pretends embarrassment, assumes stage fright: "It will be courting ridicule for an amateur like me to improvise on the same theme as an accomplished writer." But Phaedrus, of course, is not taken in by this coyness; indeed, the whole conversation has not been serious; the whole thing is a game, a rhetorical sporting event. Everyone in Athens knows this game. It is in these terms, I think, that Phaedrus misunderstands what is taking place.

Incidentally, this whole interlude is done with sparkling vivacity, one pun coming hard upon the next. We would be tempted to speak of the style of Shakespearean comedies, if it were not the other way around, Shakespeare probably having learned a few tricks in the school of Platonic dialogue. When, for example, Phaedrus says that he wants to set up a golden statue, Socrates replies at once: "Oh, what a golden boy you are!" Which is to say: You talk like someone left over from the Golden Age; you're of legendary simplicity! [1] We must appreciate such details as the philologists have discovered for us, in order to realize the rich references Plato's language had for his contemporary readers.

Finally Phaedrus threatens his recalcitrant companion with simple force: "We are by ourselves in a lonely place, and I am stronger and younger than you . . . please don't

236
d 4

235
e 2

236
c 8

3 0

make me use force to open your lips." And then he adds a more convincing argument: "I have something to say which will compel you to speak." — "Then please don't say it." — "Oh, but I shall, here and now; and what I say will be on oath. I swear to you by—but by whom, by what god? Or shall it be by this plane tree? I swear that unless you deliver your speech here in its very presence, I will assuredly never again declaim nor report any other speech by any author whatsoever." — "Aha, you rogue!" And so on. All this is pure comedy. And Socrates seems to be carrying his joke to its climax when he covers his head so
he can rush through his speech "without looking at you and breaking down for shame."

Afterwards, however, Socrates will give a completely different interpretation of this gesture, will speak of it as a token of religious awe and shame over the blasphemous things he is about to say. For Socrates the content, the truth or falsehood, remains the decisive and serious aspect of a speech; Phaedrus, on the other hand, expects to hear him outdo Lysias' formal accomplishment. To be sure, Socrates diligently fosters this misunderstanding.

Socrates, then, begins his speech. It, too, is a courtship speech as was agreed. Right at the beginning, however, a difference between it and Lysias' speech becomes apparent, a difference which extends also to the realm of form. In Lysias' speech, the speaker himself and his actual intention remained obscure. Socrates begins by clearly identify-
ing the speaker: "Once upon a time there was a very handsome boy, or rather youngster, who had a host of lovers; and one of them was wily, and had persuaded the boy that he was not in love with him, though really he was, quite as much as the others. And on one occasion, in pressing his

suit he actually sought to convince him that he ought to favor a non-lover rather than a lover. And this is the purport of what he said . . ." Then follows the courtship speech itself. It is clear, then, that it is not Socrates himself who is speaking, but someone who wants to deceive, a wily cheat who not only lies but lies for his own ulterior purpose. This cheat, moreover, speaks much more bluntly, much more consistently, than the speaker of Lysias' speech.

237
d 3

"Both desire, the lover as well as the non-lover. How then are we to distinguish the one from the other?" Now Lysias definitely did not want to talk so plainly, while Socrates by his very directness means to expose the absurdity and inhumanity of the argument. He amplifies and exaggerates. Being in love, love, shattering erotic emotion —all these are nothing but naked desire, linked with inconsiderateness and uselessness. Only the non-lover can be considerate and reasonable; he alone can do right. So the argument runs.

Karl Joel [2] has commented that possibly this can or must be understood as a parodistic allusion to the doctrines of the Cynics, such as were advocated by Antisthenes, a companion of Plato, who claimed to derive them from Socrates. In that case the speech, and above all its recantation, would acquire an unexpected contemporaneity for us. For Antisthenes is an astoundingly modern figure; he might be called the first embodiment of the "worker." [3] Here for the first time we find set forth an ideal characterized by over-evaluation of difficulty and effort; by the lack of a receptivity to art; by inadequate responsiveness to love— for emotion is regarded as weakness. Such an ideal in fact seems like a forerunner of the modern functionary, in whose world there is only heroic noise, but no music; only discipline, but no free flow; only manly "bearing," but no natural, unforced gestures; and, consistently, only the naked brutishness of sex separated from love. It is quite possible that Plato's Socrates means to portray just such a type. This, however, can scarcely be proved; for the whole treatment of the subject is so thoroughly a parody.

We shall have to imagine the tone in which this speech is delivered as a combination of pedantry and high-sounding bathos. Socrates begins like a schoolmaster, with broad, complacent hairsplitting. He himself calls attention to the bathetic quality of his remarks; after he has finished saying grandiloquently that love is nothing but overpowering desire which gains mastery over judgment, he interrupts himself, and presumably peering out from under his cloak asks: "Well, Phaedrus my friend, do you think as I do that I am divinely inspired?" Whereupon Phaedrus, failing to notice the acute irony, replies: "Undoubtedly, Socrates, you have been vouchsafed a quite unusual eloquence." — "Then listen to me in silence," Socrates commands. "For truly there seems to be a divine presence in this spot, so that you must not be surprised if, as my speech proceeds, I become as one possessed; already my style is not far from dithyrambic." — "Very true," Phaedrus says. —"But for that you are responsible. Still, let me continue. . . ."

Anyone who fails to notice the element of comedy in this is, I fear, beyond help.[4] At the end it emerges even more plainly. Socrates grows tired of the pose. He has wound up his speech by railing against lovers after the manner of Lysias, or perhaps of the Cynic Antisthenes, insisting that love is not love at all, but hunger, animal appetite; "as wolf to lamb, so lover to his lad." And then he abruptly breaks off: "There you have it, Phaedrus. Not a word more shall you have from me."

Phaedrus objects that he is only halfway through; that he still has to deliver a paean to the non-lover. "Why is it, Socrates, that instead you break off?" Whereupon Socrates once more points out the bombast and bathos of his speech:

241
e 1

"My dear good man, haven't you noticed that I've got beyond dithyramb, and am breaking out into epic verse, despite my faultfinding? What do you suppose I shall do if I start extolling the other type? Don't you see I shall clearly be possessed. . . ."

But let us consider Socrates' speech as a whole, and ask what its *content* signifies. Friedländer, it seems to me, gives an excellent and completely accurate analysis of that content. Socrates' speech, he says, "is by no means merely a re-editing and formal revision of the speech of Lysias. Rather, it is simultaneously a working out of the human significance which was vaguely, and therefore all the more dangerously, implicit in Lysias' Sophistic production. Until the implicit dangers have been brought to light, Socrates cannot fight them. In his speech, therefore, the speaker shows by every word he says what a low view he takes of love. . . . In other words, instead of making a direct attack upon an attitude governed by unsavory eroticism, Socrates merely voices that attitude in such a way that it exposes itself. That is the burden of Socrates' first speech." [5] The effect of Socrates' speech is to unmask the "speaker" by taking him at his word.

Socrates stops abruptly. With some brusqueness, he tells Phaedrus that he has now spoken enough. "I will take myself off across the river here before you drive me to greater lengths." — "Oh, but not now, in the scorching noonday

242
a 1

heat!" Phaedrus exclaims in dismay. Socrates yields to this argument. However, having from one moment to the next become deadly serious, he adduces an altogether different reason: "At the moment when I was about to cross the river, dear friend, there came to me my familiar divine sign—which always checks me when on the point of doing something or other. . . ."

A great deal has been written about the Socratean *daimonion*. Socrates' own account of it, especially in his *Apology*, is the most authoritative: "You have heard me speak of it many times; the divine voice has been constantly with me all through my life till now, opposing me in quite small matters if I were not going to act rightly; . . . sometimes it has stopped me in the middle of a speech; but today, although I was on my way to court, to the death sentence, it has been silent—because . . . what has happened to me is a good" (40 a–b). If we consider this and similar explanations from Socrates himself, we cannot concur with those interpreters who hold that the daimon was simply *conscience*. Rather, we must consider it as a phenomenon belonging to the oracular realm [6]—though that, of course, makes its nature no clearer. In any case, this oracular sign now comes to Socrates: "I seemed to hear a voice forbidding me to leave the spot until I had made atonement for some offense to heaven. . . . I understand already well enough what my offense was."

242
b 8

242
d 2

Here Socrates is bandying terms which unequivocally belong to the sphere of religion: the daimonic sign; offense to the divine; atonement; the soul as seer which recognizes its own errors; he himself needs to atone and he clearly realizes his *harmartema*, which means nothing more nor less than "sin."

"What are you saying?" Phaedrus asks, and Socrates replies that both speeches were terrible, the one Phaedrus brought with him and the one he compelled Socrates to make. "How so?" Phaedrus asks. And Socrates answers: "They were foolish and somewhat blasphemous; and what could be more terrible than that?"

At last Socrates is speaking for himself. True pathos breaks through, and with an angry gesture he sweeps aside the equivocations of rank pleasure-seeking. Irony, laughter, and finally the lightning of blunt language have cleared the air. They have made room for the only subject which Plato really thinks worth discussing, and which is now taken up: a meditation upon love and erotic emotion considered in terms of the whole of human existence. And an essential part of that whole is that life is not defined solely in terms of the all-too-human, the nothing-but-human.

IV

*The Kierkegaardian Reversal: evocation of the aesthetic leads to re-
ligious truth.   The power of recantation and repentance.   "Love
among free men."   The emergence of the images of the gods.   The
masquerade goes on.*

By the time we have reached the present point in the dialogue, we may well feel ourselves thwarted by the unremit-
ting irony, the obscurities and ambiguities of the masquerade, and the constant necessity to reappraise what has
just been said. We may begin to wonder whether we have
succeeded in clarifying the matter under discussion and
whether we have really made any progress. Let us then
sum up our findings: We have heard Lysias' speech on the
theme of Love, a speech which represents the voice of the
enlightened, avant-garde intelligentsia. His statement, cast
in choice and polished diction, is based on a rationalistic
view of life as a "technique," which attempts to secure a
maximum of pleasure with a minimum of "complications."
The language draws a veil over the real impulse: naked
desire directed purely toward pleasure, in the most unsavory sense of that word. This is disguised as objectivity,
consideration, and decency. On the other hand, the shattering emotion which is the natural accompaniment of
love appears, in Lysias' speech, as romanticism, exaggera-

tion, unnecessary upheaval in a sensible, temperate existence, ethically questionable, and in fact basically immoral.
No doubt such "theories" were widely discussed among the
younger generation in Plato's Athens. Such arguments
must have enjoyed wide publicity, whereas the Socratic-
Platonic doctrine must have seemed hopelessly esoteric by
comparison, limited to a very small circle, without wide
appeal or influence. The whole tone of Lysias' discourse
on the theme of Love is the superior, self-assured tone of
a "modernist." Its author knows that it will arouse immediate echo and applause among those who are "intellectually alive." Sure enough, Phaedrus, a representative
of the intellectually alive younger generation, enthusiastically hails this speech by the ablest writer of the
age. He and his fellows are sure they are the avant-garde.
And Socrates, so utterly of different mind that he cannot
even accept the way the question is posed, ironically capit-
ulating before the carelessness with which Phaedrus swal-
lows wholesale these impossible, inhuman, destructive
ideas—Socrates attempts to expose the absurdity of such
doctrines by taking them at their word and pursuing them
to their ultimate consequences. He attempts this, but the
attempt fails. Phaedrus simply fails to notice; even Socrates' preposterous speech strikes him as wonderful, or at
least "interesting" and important. Enthralled as he is
chiefly by literary quality, he at the very least considers
it a respectable rival performance. Until finally Socrates
loses patience with him.

And now Socrates speaks for himself—sharply, unspar-
ingly, without any concern for what the followers of fashionable ideas might expect of him. We witness something
which Sören Kierkegaard two thousand years later—citing

Socrates, incidentally—defined as the underlying principle of his life as a writer: "to beguile a person into the truth." [1] In this Kierkegaard sees the *maieutic* or midwife's function of the writer's art: ". . . he [the religious writer] must have everything in readiness, though without impatience, with a view to bringing forward the religious promptly, as soon as he perceives that he has his readers with him, so that with the momentum gained by devotion to the aesthetic they rush headlong into contact with the religious." [2]

We have reached the point in the dialogue at which Socrates performs what we might call the Kierkegaardian Reversal. He makes Phaedrus' admiration for formal eloquence rush headlong into the *religious* truth about Love. Now his whole tone and manner change. The masquerade is over; instead we hear a new note of strong emotion.

From its very outset, the second speech on Eros plainly springs from religious inspiration. All the previous verbiage is dismissed, not only as stupid and absurd, but quite explicitly as sin, as blasphemy practiced for the sake of winning praise from men—"as though it were good sense to deceive a few miserable people and win their applause." But what Socrates is going to say now will be more than correction or even recantation; *it will be atonement*. "I have to purify myself."

It should be noted that completely new elements are being introduced here. Wilamowitz calls this second speech of Socrates, which actually begins in the dialogue, a "foreign body," [3] even stylistically. That is scarcely an exaggeration. When, however, Wilamowitz goes on to say that the "mood of nature" has inspired Socrates to "divine madness," he is obscuring the decisive factor. Granting Socrates' repeated references to the divinities of the country-side, of the spring, of the shady spot under the plane tree, we miss the true meaning of such language if we take it as mere phraseology, the idle remarks of an educated mind. Nowadays, of course, we may speak of nymphs and of the Muses without attributing any substantial reality to them; the words are mere cultural tags. But that was not the case with Socrates.

It should be apparent that the concepts of sacrilege and sin are necessarily tied to the concept of divinity. Strictly speaking, sin is directed against God. There is no real sinning against man. Socrates and Plato are as aware of that as the author of the *Miserere* psalm (Ps. 50, 6). The reason Socrates speaks of sacrilege, sin, godlessness, is stated in so many words: "Love is a god or something divine."

The ideas of expiation, atonement, and purification, however, pertain not just to religion alone, but to religious *ritual* in the strict sense: the cleansing of those impurities which exclude a person from ritual. The Greeks also thought of expiation as primarily a rite, such as washing in flowing water or in the sea: "The sea rinses away all the evil of man." [4] On the other hand, such ritualistic expiation was not separated from the ethical aspects of atonement, from conviction, volition, and conversion. Socrates speaks of recantation as of an old form of expiation and purification. (He comments, however, that Homer did not understand it. This is an extraordinary comment which I would not presume to explain. All the same, it may be that Socrates-Plato are implying that Homer, as was the case in his anecdotes about the gods and his picture of the dreariness of life in the other world, was scarcely respecting the sacred tradition on this point either.)

In fact recantation, "repentance" as an old mode of expiation and purification, at first glance seems a highly un-Greek idea. Nietzsche [5] leaped to this deceptive conclusion and defended it persistently and passionately. But Plato and Socrates seem to have really upheld the principle of the purifying power of repentance. Socrates appears to
243
d 4
be drawing on the same metaphor when he says that he wishes to wash the bitter taste out of his mouth with a draught of the sweet spring water of wholesome discourse. He is going to make a new speech in which he recants
243
b 5
what has been said in the two preceding speeches. "I shall attempt to make my due palinode to Love . . . and no longer veiling my head for shame, but uncovered." Thus Socrates at last gives the real reason for his strange gesture of covering his head. He had not done so out of embarrassment at attempting to compete with the expert writer Lysias, but out of *aischyne*, shame, the feeling of having done something disgraceful.

243
c 1
"Yes, dear Phaedrus: you understand how irreverent the two speeches were, the one in the book and that which followed." They were irreverent and shameful not only before the gods, but also before men; although not everyone would have felt this, but only a man of noble and sensitive character. In other words, Socrates is saying: Lysias and I spoke as though real, noble, generous love never existed; as though decency were simply a fiction, a naïve,
243
c 2
unrealistic idea. "Suppose," Socrates says, "we were being listened to by a man of generous and humane character, who loved or had once loved another such as himself . . . wouldn't he be sure to think that we had been brought up

among galley slaves and had never seen love among free men?"

Is it necessary to point out that this contrast between galley slaves and free men has nothing to do with the *social* phenomenon of slavery? In Plato (and in Aristotle also, who for example speaks of forms of music which impress slaves and animals [6]) there is a concept of slavery which no social changes, no emancipation of the slaves, can wipe off the face of the earth. This conception is rooted in the belief that what is truly human is never the average. The standard by which truth and falsehood, good and evil, are measured, is not alone the divine, but also the human. To put that more exactly: the standard is what man himself is capable of being, and what he is called upon to be. The man before whom Socrates feels shame is not just anybody. Rather, Socrates is referring to Phaedrus himself, a Phaedrus seen in the light of his true human potentialities; a Phaedrus who will have become what he was meant to become. Shamed in this sense, Socrates wishes to recant his shamefully false speech by a second speech on Love. This second speech is the real content of the dialogue; it is also what makes reading the rest worth while.

I have gone to such pains to analyze the preliminaries to Socrates' recantation in order to show the fundamental change of atmosphere that has taken place since Phaedrus, coming from the dubious company in which he met Lysias, ran across Socrates. The dialogue situation is by now under the sign of another planet, as it were. They had begun to talk under the sign of "pleasure" and "literature." Their tone was that of sophisticated indifference to what man truly is and what he truly ought to aim for. In the society which gives rise to such attitudes, men are hedged in by concern for profit and loss. They anxiously count their every advantage, weigh their stakes against their possible gains. This is the vaporous realm of wordy egotism in which men are constantly trying to get as much as they can for the lowest price. That whole pose is now shattered by Socrates' act and proclamation. Socrates steps forth from the fogs into the clear light of heaven, as it were. In place of a literary exercise, we have the genuine emotion of one who is saying what must be said. Hitherto the view has been constricted by fear of losing out on life's possible pleasures and benefits. Now the images of the gods emerge, and along with them the true potentialities of man himself. We find ourselves breathing fresher, cooler, purer air.

The masquerade recedes, as we have said; but it does not entirely vanish. Plato is careful to avoid the monotony of high-flown professions of faith. Socrates is rarely shown holding forth in such a vein; for that very reason, his seriousness reveals itself all the more distinctly and movingly as it alternates with more or less ironic masquerade. The austerity of solemn speechmaking is at once tempered and highlighted by an anecdote which is playfully turned this way and that. Socrates recounts the legend of the Sicilian poet Stesichorus, who told the story of Helen—whom the Dorians regarded as a goddess—in the same way Homer had told it. Whereupon he was punished—by the *goddess* Helen—with blindness. But because Stesichorus was a "*daimonic*" man, a familiar of the Muses, he understood the reason for his blindness, and after writing a "recantation" found his sight restored to him. We are not concerned here with the details of this anecdote and its possible historical background. But we are concerned with the fact that Socrates is now playing the part of Stesichorus, who has lost his sight and hopes to be healed if he in turn makes a recantation. To point out the multiple allusions of this new masquerade, the wealth of associations hinted at in a gesture "performed" casually and briefly, is to run the risk of coarsening or altogether destroying the delicacy of the texture.

243
e 4 "Where is that boy?" Socrates asks like a blind man calling for his companion. But at the same time he means the boy he addressed before, and on the other hand he is speaking not as himself, Socrates, but as another, a perfidious deceiver. "Where is that boy I was talking to? He must listen to me once more, and not rush off to yield to his non-lover." Moreover, strictly speaking, neither the boy who guides the blind man, nor the one to whom the previous blasphemous speech was directed, is actually meant; the one who is meant, but not mentioned by name, is Phaedrus! And Phaedrus, at once understanding, plays along: "Here he is, quite close beside you, whenever you want him."

Nevertheless, Socrates begins his speech in such a way that he is talking about Phaedrus as if he were someone altogether different, a stranger not present at all—as if, in fact, he were dealing with two Phaedruses, one of whom, the true Phaedrus, is listening to him now, and the other of whom invented that "magnificent" discourse by Lysias and provoked Socrates himself into delivering a blasphemous speech against Love.

243
e 9 The first sentence of the great speech Socrates now launches upon goes: "Now you must understand, fair boy, that whereas the preceding discourse was by Phaedrus, son of Pythocles, of Myrrinous, that which I shall now pronounce . . ." We would expect this sentence to end:

". . . not only pretends, like the last speech, to be mine, but really is mine." Instead it continues: ". . . that which I shall now pronounce is by Stesichorus, son of Euphemus, of Himera. This then is how it must run . . ." And now follows the recantation, the *palinodia*.

It begins with the word "no." But negation is only the first word. The affirmative thesis quickly follows.

V

Mania as a divine gift.   Madness, loss of autonomous self-possession, passio, enthusiasm.   Forms of "divine madness."   First: prophetic ecstasy: Delphi, Dodona, the Sibyl.   Sterility of the historical point of view.   Enthusiasm, the key word.   How does revelation take place?   Second: "cathartic" mania.   Madness as precondition for purification and healing.   Frenzy, poetry, and inspiration.   Lessing, Hölderlin, Goethe, Benn.   Who is "the poet"?

244
a 6 "The greatest blessings come by way of *mania,* insofar as *mania* is heaven-sent." This pronouncement of Socrates unquestionably forms the very heart of the whole dialogue. For the moment we shall leave the basic word *mania* untranslated. The sentence is aimed not only against Lysias' hypothesis, which Socrates pretended to echo in his parody of Lysias' speech; it is also aimed against the ideas currently in vogue in Athenian society.

The new thesis contains within itself a whole view of the universe. Above all, it sets forth a fundamental opinion on the meaning of human existence. The subject of Love, which previously formed the central theme of the discourse, is not even mentioned. This at first glance rather astonishing silence is in line with the fact that the discussion has been shifted to new and wider perspectives. But if we are to be prepared to accept, or even merely to follow, the far-reaching argumentation which now begins, we must first clarify in our own minds just what was the "blasphemous" element in the preceding speeches on Love.

For both those speeches are in the nature of conclusions. That is to say, they are the "application" of a larger doctrine concerning the nature of man. And Socrates takes issue with that doctrine and propounds his own thesis concerning man and the meaning of his life.

His first step is to break down a nonsensical restriction. The fashionable Sophistic "publicists" have done their best to focus their readers' thought and attention upon a superficial theory of "flirtation," so to speak. Socrates refuses even to enter the arena of such discussions—not because he wishes to avoid the subject of Eros, but because he wants to place that subject in its only appropriate context. Therefore his attack is directed against the general view of man which holds, among other things, that the right approach toward sensual gratification is one of cool objectivity. To put that general conception in a nutshell, it is that man is a completely autonomous being whose own nature is given into his hand like a raw material which may be worked in any manner he pleases; a being who determines his own purposes; who himself arranges his existence by rational techniques for living, and whose dignity therefore demands that he fend off any interference with this realm of perfect self-possession—whatever the source of that interference may be. This picture of man is what Socrates attacks in the speech that follows. His opposition to any such conception of man is the key which alone explains what he has to say.

Socrates, then, does not contend that Eros is not *mania*; but he denies that *mania* itself is simply an evil, a "sickness," as the Sophists call it, in the jargon of their techniques for living. We cannot say whether something is or is not a sickness until we have determined what we mean by health. And this is where Socrates and his opponents differ so widely in their views of human soundness. His statement, however, is rather subtle. Socrates does not maintain that *mania* is normal to man and essential to his soundness. Rather, he says that it is not an evil in every case. Nor does he outrightly declare *mania* a good. Instead, he says that it can possibly be a means, an aid, a path to a good, in fact even to the greatest blessings—on condition, that is, that *mania* is imparted to man as a divine gift.

But what is meant by *mania*? The word is often translated *frenzy* or *madness*. But "madness" seems to me an inadequate and misleading definition. In the first place, the word connotes unsoundness and irrationality. In the second place, it gives the impression that Socrates is talking about something from the realm of primitive magic. It suggests ties with the orgiastic Dionysian cults. This in effect makes his ideas seem alien and of no serious concern to us. The term *frenzy*, on the other hand, suggests something poetic, romantic, non-essential, something that may even be arbitrarily induced by a drug; once again, ideas of this sort need not really concern us. We do not have to take them seriously.

If we consider all the aspects of *mania* which Plato mentions, we shall have to say that he uses the word to mean, primarily, a being-beside-oneself, a loss of command over oneself, surrender of autarchic independence and self-control; a state in which we are not active, but passive. We do not act, but suffer something; something happens to us. French scholars, in interpreting this passage in Plato, speak of *transport*,[1] that is, a condition of being carried away out of the center of one's own being. But all these alternatives convey only one element of what Plato means: the element of weakness or, if we will, of sickness and "derangement." Yet it is also conceivable that this being-beside-oneself may not be caused by mental disturbance, not by poison or drugs, but by a divine power. The Deity is the truly active source from which something happens to man. For this very reason, we cannot speak simply of *madness* or *frenzy* without further qualifying the words. If the word *enthusiasm* were not so debased in English, it would in fact most fittingly describe what Plato intended, and indeed he himself uses it in the sense of "being filled with the god." In the middle of the *Phaedrus*, Socrates speaks of a man thus possessed by *mania*. "The multitude," he says, "regard him as being out of his wits, for they know not that he is full of a god [*enthousiazon*]."

249
d 2

Now Plato scarcely asserts that anyone who is shaken by erotic emotion is filled with the god, so that all forms of Eros are nothing more nor less than *theia mania*. Such romantic ideas are not to be found in Plato. However, Socrates' speech does maintain that erotic emotion may *also* be one way in which man can partake of "the greatest blessings"—provided man does not corrupt the erotic emotion by, for example, refusing to pay the price of receptivity to the divine madness. The price is a surrender of his autonomy; he must throw himself open to the god, rather than lock the doors of his soul by choosing sensual pleasures alone.

But before he comes to this, Socrates speaks of quite different matters. As we have said, no one will understand their pertinence who has not given due consideration to the general thesis posed at the outset. This thesis holds that on the one hand man is of such nature that he possesses himself in freedom and self-determination; he can and must examine critically all that he encounters; he can and must give shape to his own life on the basis of his insights. On the other hand this same autonomous man is nonetheless so much involved in the Whole of reality that things can happen to him and he can be dislodged from his autonomy. This need not take only the form of forcible restriction. Provided that the man does not close himself off obdurately, it may take such a form that in the very loss of his self-possession another fulfillment is granted to him, one attainable in no other way.

This conception of man, involving as it does a tension of opposites which refuses to be reduced to a smooth formula, which is in itself a perpetual source of unrest—this conception may be said to have been Plato's central problem throughout his life. To be sure, he did not always place his stress in exactly the same way. Like all those truly engaged in the pursuit of philosophy, he was not so much concerned with finding a "solution" and a handy formula; rather, he was anxious not to omit anything. Consequently, he never denied, or overlooked the fact, that both autonomy and the shattering of that autonomy by the intrusion of a higher power are essential to the nature of man. But he was not always disposed to regard the relinquishing of self-possessed autonomy as a gain. In the early dialogues *Ion* and *Meno*, as well as in Socrates' *Apology*, he seems to be emphasizing the idea of loss rather than gain. Poets and those in manic frenzy do not know what they are saying; they speak the truth, but not on the basis of real knowledge which, if they had it, would be their own property, at their own disposal—and so on. So runs the argument. Thus Plato himself in these early remarks seems inclined to call *mania* a sickness, although he would have declared it an even worse sickness not to be able to be "sick" in such a way. ("The sickness which consists of being unable to be sick"—this phrase, straight out of the lexicon of modern psychiatry, would not be a bad description for the Sophistic self-possession we have been discussing.) Here, on the other hand, in the *Phaedrus*, both these antithetical ideas are spoken of in a tone of decided affirmation. "He had never expressed anything of the sort before," Wilamowitz notes.[2]

Socrates now begins to speak of the four different forms of the *theia mania*; and erotic emotion comes fourth rather than first.

244
a 8

In first place, he speaks of prophetic ecstasy, of divination in its narrowest sense, the *transport prophétique*. He specifically cites the prophetess of Delphi, the priestesses at Dodona, and the Sibyl. What is common to all of these is that in a state of exaltation, of being beside themselves, they accomplished great things by their prophecies, whereas while sane and in full possession of themselves they could have said nothing of importance.

In the time of Socrates, Delphi was a sanctuary already more than a thousand years old. Its prestige extended far into Asia and Egypt. Whatever we may think of some aspects of the Delphic Oracle, its influence, especially on politics, can scarcely be overestimated. The religious and ethical mandates implicit in many of its pronouncements had a force and sway whose match is scarcely to be found anywhere else in the pre-Christian world. Delphi proclaimed the sanctity of the right of asylum; Delphi set curbs upon the practice of vendetta. The Delphic Oracle also enunciated the earliest rules for humane warfare, thus establishing a kind of international law.

The priestesses of Dodona in northern Greece were the authors of the oldest specimens of Greek religious wisdom in hymnic form, a fragment of which has come down to us: "Zeus was, Zeus is, and Zeus will be: O Zeus, Thou mighty one!" [3] We all too easily tend to overlook such things while regaling ourselves with the irreverent anecdotes about the gods contained in Homeric mythology, which Plato regarded as perversions of the true—that is the *Greek*—divine doctrine.

Finally, the Sibyl. The oldest testimony we have concerning her comes from one of the greatest of the pre-Socratic philosophers, Heraclitus; it is also of Sibylline obscurity: "The Sibyl, uttering her unlaughing, unadorned, unincensed words with raving mouth, reaches out over a thousand years with her voice, through the god." [4]

For Plato's contemporaries, all these things were so familiar that Socrates explicitly states: "I need not dwell on what is obvious to everyone." And summing up, he makes the point that "the men of old who gave things their names" meant the word *mania* as praise when they used it to account for the power of prophecy possessed by the oracular priestess and the Sibyl. A few lines later this statement is reinforced: the evidence of the Ancients attests that the *theia mania*, heaven-sent madness, is more worthy of veneration than the products of human discretion.

Our first impulse, as latter-day readers of Plato, is to assign these statements about prophetic madness, about Delphi, Dodona, and the Sibyl, to the "religious history of the Greeks," and leave it at that. And if we look in the

244
b 5

244
b 6

244
d 4

scholarly literature on Plato, we will find considerable incentive for doing so. Nevertheless, if we follow this principle, we are simply cheating ourselves of the proper fruits of studying or even merely reading Plato. In this connection I cannot help thinking of C. S. Lewis's *Screwtape Letters*. A devil grown wise by long practice, here called Screwtape, writes a series of letters of instruction and advice to his less experienced nephew—the result being a treatise on man as witty as it is profound, although everything appears inverted as in mirror writing. In one of the letters Screwtape discusses the matter of studying the Ancients:

"Only the learned read old books and we [the united spirits of hell] have now so dealt with the learned that they are of all men the least likely to acquire wisdom by doing so. We have done this by inculcating The Historical Point of View. The Historical Point of View, put briefly, means that when a learned man is presented with any statement in an ancient author, the one question he never asks is whether it is true. He asks who influenced the ancient writer, and how far the statement is consistent with what he said in other books, and what phase in the writer's development, or in the general history of thought, it illustrates, and how it affected later writers, and how often it has been misunderstood (specially by the learned man's own colleagues). . . ." And so on.[5]

But suppose we pause and ask ourselves whether Plato's remarks on the first form of exalted madness strike at the heart of any real matter; whether he brings to light something which actually corresponds to the reality of man as a being. The moment we pose this question, we can no longer file Plato's statements away as merely historical items. For the question instantly breaks out of the confines of the mere past.

The contemporary Christian, for example, encounters the Sibyl in the sequence *Dies irae* of the Church's liturgy for the dead. She is mentioned in the same breath with the Biblical King David—both of whom prophetically witness to a catastrophic end to history (*teste David cum Sibylla*). Perhaps the contemporary Christian sees the allusion as a mere flourish without any particular meaning to him. But if we are seriously interested in understanding Plato's reference to the Sibyl, we must make a stronger effort to translate what he said and meant into the terms of our own thinking. Incidentally, we can draw upon one such "translation," a pre-Christian one, into a language rather closer to us, the Latin of the Romans. In the sixth book of the *Aeneid*, which describes how Aeneas questions the Sibyl of Cumae, the *theia mania* emerges as real "holy raving." In the vast, hundred-mouthed grotto of Cumae "issue a hundred voices"; the Sibyl herself stands by the threshold —"suddenly nor countenance nor color was the same, nor stayed her tresses braided; but her bosom heaves, her heart swells with wild frenzy, and she is taller to behold, nor has her voice a mortal ring, since now she feels the nearer breath of the god." [6] "So does Apollo shake the reins as she rages, and ply the spur beneath her breast." [7]

But graphic as the passage is, it is not what I would call a translation into terms familiar to us. The real clue lies in a single word of Virgil's. The word is used in the first verses of Book VI, in which he says of the Sibyl that the Delian god, Apollo, "breathed into her a great mind and soul." This breathing in is called *inspiratio*—our word inspiration.[8]

With the help of this word, we can now more clearly rephrase the statement made in the *Phaedrus*. Human nature is so placed within its plane of existence that it remains essentially open to the sphere of the divine. Man is so constituted that, on the one hand, he can be thrown out of the autonomous independence of his thinking by *inspiration*, which comes to him as a sudden, unpredictable force from outside. On the other hand, this very abandonment of critical sovereignty may bring him an abundance of insight, of light, of truth, of illumination as to the nature of reality which would otherwise remain completely out of his reach. For we are dealing not with self-governing human genius, but with something bestowed by another, a higher, a divine power. Nor is this merely an abstract possibility: man's being *is* at times overpowered by inspiration. It is something that actually happens. But when it does happen, it does so in such a manner that *sophrosyne* and all that goes with that is forcibly annulled, however much the dignity of the human person depends upon it. Inspiration takes the form of *theia mania*, of the self's not-being-with-the-self—so that the state of being inspired may well seem madness to the "multitude."

It at once becomes clear that such a statement calls for an inquiry into the metaphysical structure of the human being. This is a subject which can scarcely be grasped "scientifically." Anyone who wishes to enter such a discussion must be prepared to "declare" ultimate positions. Put briefly and bluntly, this means that a Christian concerned with a philosophical interpretation of Plato cannot, when faced with such sentences, avoid bringing the Christian creed into the discussion. And it need scarcely be said that he would altogether concur with Plato in holding that the limitations of human nature and its infinite openness and receptivity—both together—are manifest in the experience of revelatory divine inspiration.

The question remains, to be sure, whether this agreement would also extend to the manner of revelation and inspiration. Could a Christian theologian accept the Platonic concept of "enthusiastic" ecstasy and *mania,* however often it is called *divine* madness? In what way, exactly, does Christian theology conceive that revelation and inspiration came to the first recipient? I confess that I would have expected a more temperate, more prudent, rationally cooler account. What was my astonishment when I looked in Thomas Aquinas, who certainly cannot be charged with lack of sobriety, and came upon a description of the process of revelation virtually the same as that contained in Plato's *Phaedrus.* In speaking of revelation and inspiration as they come to man, Thomas uses the words *prophetia* and *raptus.* The very word *raptus,* with its connotation of coercion and force, is not so far from *theia mania.* This implication is strengthened by the Scholastic definition Thomas quotes: being raised up by a higher power—away from what is proper to nature, toward what is contrary to nature (*in id quod est contra naturam*).[9] But prophecy, too, understood as an event *within* the mind of one who is being granted revelation and inspiration, is described by Thomas in terms not only of *passio* but even of failure. He asks, for example, whether *prophetia* is a *habitus,* something that the "prophet" possesses as a property, a gift, an ability.[10] His answer is: No, the prophetic light is present in the soul of the prophet in the manner of suffering, or a "fleeting scratch." "To be sure, prophecy, insofar as it is seeing on the prophet's part, is in some sense a spiritual act; but in regard to the light that suddenly is received and is like something passing through ('like sunlight in the atmosphere' [11]), it resembles suffering." [12] "In prophetic revelation the spirit of the prophet is stirred by the Holy Spirit like a failing tool. . . ." [13] Finally, quite unexpectedly we find Thomas, who usually manifests such sober rationality, saying that the cognition of the sleeper is more powerfully receptive than that of the waker [14]—thus taking the surprising step of coming fully over to the side of Plato. Both these types of cognition, however, cannot be attained or comprehended by rationalism, which renders a false picture of the Whole of life.

The second form of god-induced ecstasy which Socrates discusses has been termed, in an abbreviated formula, "cathartic *mania*." [15] If we are to come to terms with anything that we ourselves regard as truth, we must naturally hold *some* opinion on the subject under discussion. And at first glance that precondition seems absent here. What, then, is meant by "cathartic *mania*"? First of all, what is said about it? The text reads as follows: "When grievous maladies and afflictions have beset certain families by reason of some ancient sin, *mania* has appeared amongst them, and breaking out into prophecy has secured relief by finding the means thereto, namely by recourse to prayer and worship; and in consequence thereof rites and means of purification were established, and the sufferer was brought out of danger, alike for the present and the future. Thus did madness secure, for him that was maddened aright and possessed, deliverance from his troubles."

Plato scholarship has little to say about this text. Wilamowitz is frank about his own reaction to the passage:

244
d 5

"This remains incomprehensible" [16]; "I have not found an explanation anywhere, and I myself remain perplexed." [17]

Of course we might recommend simply leaving the passage aside—if it were not disturbing to find ourselves completely unable to see any meaning, that is to say, any distinct reference to reality, in a thesis which Plato is obviously presenting with great earnestness. Disturbing not so much because we are faced with an enigma of the sort resented by historians and students of literature, but because we would begin to worry about our blind spot. For we should really know what Plato is talking about when he makes so definite a statement and plainly thinks it a matter of first importance.

There are two questions to be raised here. First: In the whole body of our present knowledge of man, is there anything corresponding to what Plato calls "grievous maladies and afflictions . . . by reason of some ancient sin"? Some translations put that: "stemming from an ancient curse" (K. Hildebrandt, for example). *Menima* in fact means both: sin (or guilt) and wrath (the wrath of the gods).

Secondly, we must ask: Is there anything in our picture of man which corresponds to what Plato says about god-sent *mania*, namely, that it alone can deliver a man from his troubles? For only by such a parallel can we comprehend what Plato is talking about; only then can we weigh his statements against our own sense of the truth.

Before we consider the first question, let us agree that obviously the maladies, afflictions, burdens, trials, and troubles of which Plato is speaking are not—or not primarily—to be understood as *physical* maladies, sufferings, and wounds. They are *psychic* burdens which weigh upon the mind and soul. Hackforth in his commentary on *Phaedrus* remarks that Plato probably had in mind some variation of the story of Orestes, who was pursued by the spirits of vengeance, the Eumenides.[18] But the Eumenides are not only indigenous to classical tragedy. The contemporary theatergoer will also come across them in T. S. Eliot's *Family Reunion*, where they appear as a chorus stepping out of the window embrasure of a modern English country house: ". . . whether in Argos or England / There are certain inflexible laws / Unalterable, in the nature of music." But, of course, correspondence in matter is more valuable than correspondence in vocabulary. And the discoveries of modern psychoanalysis yield just such correspondences. The material which psychoanalysis has brought to light is not new and unprecedented. Rather, its insights have by and large merely confirmed the things that great knowers of the human heart, and the traditional wisdom of the race, have always known and said. And among the things psychoanalysis confirms is this: that there really are maladies and afflictions in the life of the soul which demonstrably stem from "ancient sins" or "old guilts," in which the affected individual and the preceding generations are indivisibly implicated and in which, furthermore (though this is hard to grasp concretely), a perverseness of will coincides with the inexorable fatality that comes from outside. In short, a view of man which comprehends the Whole of existence seems to suggest, in our time as much as in Plato's day, that such afflictions from such origins are indeed a reality. It suggests furthermore that man obviously cannot free himself from these afflictions by a rational technique for living; that, on the contrary, any attempt to do so will aggravate the affliction. Deliverance can be obtained, if at all, only by a process of healing which is at any rate negative—one whereby the seeker after healing must for a time surrender his hold of the rudder of rational self-control and autonomy. The important thing is *not* to behave actively, but to be passive, to let something happen—for example, by descending into the realm of the unconscious and the dream. Plato undoubtedly knew that Asclepian medicine was originally a *mantic* art in which the petitioner received instructions and healing in dreams.[19] But dreams are things we do not bring about ourselves. "We 'endure' the dream." This is not a sentence from an ancient philosopher; it was written by the modern psychologist, C. G. Jung.[20] He too, like Plato, speaks of the necessity for submitting to a state of being outside oneself, to *mania*, for the sake of healing and wholeness. To strengthen his case he quotes the "ancient motto of the Mysteries": "Let go of what you have; then you will receive." [21] What is to be received bears the same name in modern psychology as in Plato's: purification, *katharsis*.[22]

An objection might be raised to this attempt to draw an analogy between Plato and modern depth psychology. We may put it as follows: Even though that "letting the unconscious work," as we phrase it nowadays, may closely resemble the Platonic *mania*, the being-beside-oneself—the decisive fact remains that for Plato the madness is divine. It is a *theia mania*. And the theory of the unconscious says not a word about that.

There is some validity to this objection, insofar as it rests upon what is specifically said, or rather *not* said, in modern psychology. However, I would be inclined to answer it with a counter-question: Is there not a vital substratum, far removed from all rational techniques for living, where the psyche truly knows what it wants and what it needs,[23] where, unspoken, the possibility of such healing is at least dimly felt? In letting go of himself, man does not surrender to the purely "irrational." He surrenders to the healing darkness of his own divine origin.

But we must speak of something else. If Plato really had in mind the story of Orestes the matricide, then in speaking of afflictions stemming from ancient sin he may really have meant guilt, or meant that in addition. If so, he would also be asserting that guilt, crime, sin, cannot be extinguished and that we will not shake off their burden by rational guidance of our inner life, or by any technique for living, no matter how loftily conceived. Guilt is wiped out by a *theia mania*. Those of us who are Christians in this present age (once again ultimate positions must be taken—not only in case of assent, incidentally, but also in case of dissent!)—Christians, then, would have to take Plato's side, for the Christian, too, is convinced that sin can be wiped out only on the basis of *metanoia*, of repentance and conversion.

But *metanoia* means—first—that a man abandons the complacency of a mind which imagines itself autarchic. *Metanoia* is the very opposite of that attitude which Seneca formulated in a phrase that has retained its force across the centuries: that the fruit of philosophy is "never to repent anything." [24] Secondly, the concept of *metanoia* also suggests that such a change of mind cannot be effected by a mere act of will; that, rather, it must come to a man as a divine gift.

The third form of divine madness of which Socrates speaks is poetic *mania*, the ecstasy which comes from the

Muses, which "seizes a tender, virgin soul and stimulates it to rapt, passionate expression." This affirmative statement is followed by a negative dictum: True and great poetry is not possible unless it proceeds from divine madness. Those who want to be poets by skill alone will not receive the consecration. The poetry of the sane is brought to naught by the poetry of madness.

"How can this tribute to poetry . . . be reconciled with its condemnation in *The Republic,* where Plato would banish Homer and tragedy from his just state?" This query of Wilamowitz [25] recurs in one form or another throughout the literature on Plato. But perhaps there is no real problem here. Plato always—for example, in the dialogue *Meno,* written long before *The Republic*—distinguished the "*divine* poets" from those who had no right to the epithet. And he apparently placed Homer among those other, non-divine poets because Homer attributed ungodly things to the gods.

True poetry, then, has its origin in divine inspiration; it springs from a state of the soul which is madness rather than sanity, and moreover, a madness that is not produced by wine, poison, or drugs, but by a higher power. Poetry, if it is true poetry, springs from "enthusiasm" in the strict, original sense of the word.

Can this Platonic thesis be viewed in any but a purely historical light nowadays? Considering all our critical knowledge about the psychic and other bases of poetic production, of all artistic work in general, can we still seriously say that poetry springs from divine inspiration? By "we" I mean not only contemporary man in general, but also the Christian in particular. Can he subscribe to a thesis which places poetry on the same level as revelation and inspiration? To be sure, we can find in a biography of Rilke: "Rilke is a pure poet in the simple sense of a vessel for divine inspiration. To do justice to Rilke, one must believe that." [26] But we do not have to be either unpoetic or especially unreceptive to Rilke to regard such a statement as at least romantic exaggeration, if not outright blasphemy. Yet is not Plato saying precisely the same thing?

When such matters as these come up, we realize how much we lack a theological and philosophical doctrine of the nature of the arts, in terms of which we could examine this Platonic thesis, as well as others, with some adequacy. Of course, any such poetics couched in theological and philosophical terms would need constant reassessment. It would have to be examined anew in the light of the intellectual conditions of each epoch. And probably, just like theology and philosophy in general, the passage of time would make it an increasingly difficult discipline. Shortly before his death Reinhold Schneider remarked that he could not stop inquiring into the nature of poetry, but that in his experience "from year to year it becomes harder to find an answer." [27] Obviously, we cannot go into this question here. But at this point in our interpretation of *Phaedrus* we must allow ourselves to comment on it.

Whenever we think spontaneously about poetry (using the word in its widest sense, as the equivalent of the German *Dichtung*), one aspect of it remains immune to all "scientific" analysis and scholarly criticism, remains inviolate in spite of the superficial allures and popularity of obvious pseudo-poetry (whether it turns up in the form of literary acrobatics, of politically "engaged" propaganda, or of entertainment). That aspect remains inviolate even though we have schooled ourselves to regard such writers as Brecht and Benn in the least reverential of spirits. And that inviolate aspect of poetry quite clearly reinforces the Platonic thesis. It would seem that no amount of experience with specimens of debased poetry, no critico-analytic caustic agent, can attack and destroy that aspect. In the midst of rational preoccupation with literature, and even as the result of such rational activity of the intellect, this one aspect comes through again and again. We must strongly remind ourselves of this fact—thus countermanding our initial impulse to consider Plato's ideas as merely of historical significance, and leaving it at that.

Naturally, this particular aspect of literature is corroborated a hundredfold in the works of such poets as Novalis and Hölderlin. This is so obvious that there is scarcely need to speak of them. Nevertheless, we are stopped short by the following sentence of Hölderlin's, from his *Notes on Antigone,* in which he states with unromantic precision: "It is of enormous help to the secretly laboring soul that on the plane of highest consciousness it eludes consciousness." But it is more surprising to find so sober a thinker as Lessing saying of his own works that people do them too much honor to regard them as poetry and himself as a poet. "I do not feel the living spring within myself." [28] That thoughtful writer Adalbert Stifter spoke in a similar vein: "I have never thought of my works as poetry and would not be so arrogant. There are very few true poets in this world." [29] Goethe, so great a realist in his correspondence, was even more explicit. We actually find him using Platonic language: "The poet is truly deprived of his wits"; [30] "if he wishes to be modest he must admit that his state quite corresponds to a trance, and at bottom I do not deny that a good deal seems to me dreamlike." [31] As the "chief requirements of true poetic production" he mentions "irresistible nature, invincible inclination, impetuous passion." [32] What is that if not a definition of the poetic *mania* of which Plato speaks in the *Phaedrus*?

We need not, however, only go back to the past. A contemporary poet like Gottfried Benn was fond of smashing romantic halos with a rude gesture and a dash of Berlin lingo ("a poem very seldom 'arises'; a poem is *made*"). [33] But Benn, too, was fully aware of the irrational and inevitable coercion in the performance of the poetic act. In spite of many remarks directly to the contrary, he unmistakably referred to the *theia mania* aspect of poetry, to a madness stemming from (at least) a superhuman realm: "The essence of poetry is perfection and fascination"; "that it is a perfection in terms of itself, I do not maintain." [34] To be sure, we are inclined to smile at the high-flown rhetoric of Max Rychner in his epilogue to Gottfried Benn's *Selected Letters*: "His evening recourse to the dimly animated solitude of a low bar had as its aim incantation, in which the abstracted drinker became a mystagogue, his beer glass a chalice." [35] Nevertheless, this may well be a truthful account of the inner reality.

Above all, however, I must speak of a recent work of criticism in which, suddenly and quite unexpectedly, the Platonic thesis of the poet's *theia mania* abruptly rises to the surface. I am referring to a published lecture by Wolfgang Kayser entitled "Who Narrates the Novel?" [36] The focus, here, is on the true, the poetic subject of the novel. Professor Kayser's answer, arrived at through subtle structural analysis, is first of all negative: "The narrator is *not* the author." By author he means the historical individual whose name stands on the title page of the novel and whose "life" can be found in a biographical dictionary. This author, Kayser holds, is not really the narrator of the novel. Who then? He is one who "with more than human capacity sees the past as present"; [37] "a knower . . . who reveals to us . . . the permanent aspects in the order of the universe"; [38] "the narrator can do what is reserved to God and the gods alone." [39] Although this carefully reasoned conclusion is derived from study of the novel, that is, of a form not poetically "pure," and although Kayser does not fully amplify his conclusion (for fear, apparently, of finding himself face to face with overly theological categories), he has expounded something that recalls Plato's thesis. We are once again called upon to consider its pertinence to the present time.

Finally, here is a point everyone can check from his own experience. The moment we encounter the note of true poetry in the works of Gottfried Benn or Franz Kafka or Georges Bernanos, the moment we feel ourselves directly affected, we know that we are not bowing low before the Berlin dermatologist, Dr. Benn, or the two insurance clerks, Kafka and Bernanos. The now old-fashioned ornamental prefatory phrase to quotations—"as the poet says"—is not so far off the track. To be sure, who can "the poet" be, if not Dr. Benn, the dermatologist? Naturally, we will not go so far as to speak bluntly of a *divine* voice speaking through the poet's own. But could we very confidently assert that the power of great poetry to stir the soul has no connection whatsoever with the ultimate, all-embracing, divine Ground of the universe?

This is the question that Plato's statement about the poet's divine *mania* challenges us to consider.

VI

True possession of life can be had only by being "out of one's wits."
The fourth form of theia mania: erotic emotion. Nature and destiny
of the soul. Immortality. Acquiring wings. "Permeating the
whole cosmos." Figurative language as a manifestation of intellectual
humility. Parable and myth. The fall of the soul. Yearning
and recollection. Supremely beloved and supremely troubling:
beauty. "Beauty is not so much performance as promise" (Goethe).
The erotic nature of philosophizing. Forms and deformities of Eros.

Socrates seems to have wandered hopelessly far from the
original subject of Love, which alone interests young Phaedrus. He seems to be talking about something entirely beside the point—prophecy, revelatory inspiration, the healing catharsis which can be accorded us in dream and in
metanoia, poetry and the poetic state of the soul. Nevertheless, the logical connection with the starting point, with
the theme of Eros, is quite clear and firm.

This is the chain of reasoning: Do I understand that you
charge the lover with "not having his wits about him"?
Why, if that were a reproach, it would apply not only to
the lover. Do you realize how much you would be remov-
ing from the sphere of human existence if you accepted
such a charge as a genuine reproach? You would have to
rule out revelatory inspiration, for example; for the person

who receives it is "out of his wits." Yet he is partaking of something—not only for himself but for all of humanity—which cannot be gained by the most conscientious efforts of the "sound" mind. You would also be barring the healing of the soul from the fatalities which afflict it; for only those who can abandon rational self-control and autarchy, and who know how to "lose their wits," are able to experience such healing and purification. And poets, too, are out of their wits; but that is the only way that true and great poetry arises. If, then, you acknowledge that all this—receptivity to God's speech; liberating and purifying conversion, *metanoia*; the stirring of the soul by the rationally incomprehensible and ungovernable power of art—if you acknowledge that all these things constitute the true wealth of man, you agree that *mania*, madness, enthusiasm, are not at variance with the dignity of man but are, instead, essential to a truly human life. You have already taken a position against the apparent rationality of the practitioners of "techniques for living" who scorn enthusiasm. For such people are concerned with nothing more than successful gratification of human wants. They especially want that gratification to be easily manipulated and protected as much as possible from unforeseen intrusions—no matter whether the desires involved are economic or sensual or "intellectual" in nature.

Here we have matters of immense contemporary pertinence. To appreciate that, we need only consider the type of man who is already manifesting his presence, the type who says: We don't need any superhuman messages; we will take care of the purification of psychic afflictions ourselves; "arts" which serve neither the gratification of wants nor the political and technical domination of the

world are undesirable. So it is recurrently necessary to re-
vive Socrates' line of argument, and particularly in this age
of ours. That realm of existence in which theology, the
purification of the psyche by *non*-assertiveness, and all the
arts are ultimately rooted must be protected. All this must
be defended by constantly renewed educational efforts—
defended against the attempt, or, should we say, against
the temptation, to establish the self-governance and sovereign autonomy of man, his dominance of the universe and
himself, even at the cost of his forfeiting the true richness
of his life. That true richness, in the form of revelation,
of salvation, of *katharsis*, of shattering emotion that throws
open the doors of the inner self, can be had only in divine
madness, in *mania*.

This is the point at which Socrates links his discussion
of *mania* with the initial subject of Love. It remains to be
proved, he says, that the shattering emotion of love does
not similarly subject man to the experience of healing, enrichment, in fact of divinity—or at least throw open the
possibility of such experience.

This is Plato's own thesis. He does not claim that any
given infatuation of Jack and Jill, no matter what its
nature, is *eo ipso* a gift of the gods. But he does say that
in all erotic emotion something is intended for man, becomes attainable by him and accessible to him, which goes
far beyond what appears on the surface. What is intended
for him really becomes his only on condition that the impulse received in emotion is accepted and maintained with
purity. Of course there are always insidious dangers of
corruption, falsification, camouflage, disguise, pseudo-ful-
fillment. That also holds, incidentally, for prophetic, ca-

thartic, and poetic *mania*. False affirmation is a good deal worse and more barren than simple negation; sham emotions can take on a deceptive resemblance to real ones. They may even deceive those who profess them, who may think they are ecstatic over beauty when in reality they are involved in wholly unemotional, calculating pleasure-seeking. Nevertheless, Plato holds, the true lover is destined to receive a gift which may well be compared with the gift conferred upon men in divine revelation, in catharsis, and in poetic inspiration. Goethe, after speaking of his own erotic experience in *Dichtung und Wahrheit*, made the same point: "The genuine erotic leanings of uncorrupted youth take an absolutely spiritual turn. Nature seems to desire one sex to perceive goodness and beauty sensuously embodied in the other sex. And so the sight of this girl, because of my affection for her, opened up to me a new world of beauty and excellence." [1] It is a bad sign if desire precedes and therefore smothers erotic emotion. "As soon as sensuality intervenes, love cannot demand permanence," André Gide comments in his *Journals*.[2]

245
c 1
The purpose of the whole speech that follows is to show this—although right at the outset, Socrates remarks that what he is going to say will sound credible to the wise, incredible to the "efficient." In Greek the word is *deinós*, which the dictionaries define as "fearful, terrible, mighty" and "powerful, efficient, unusual." Obviously, Plato means to convey something that is at once admirable, amazing, and terrifying, and this in fact can properly be attributed to the "cleverness of the clever." Clever people, Socrates says, will find it unbelievable that in being out of their wits true lovers are being accorded a divine gift.

Now, however, Socrates once more starts from the beginning, and once more the subject of Love seems to drop hopelessly out of sight. "Now our first step towards attaining the truth of the matter," he says, "is to discern the nature of the soul, divine and human, its experiences and its activities." Someone else in the Platonic dialogues once began a speech on Eros in this fashion—namely, Aristophanes in the *Symposium*. There Aristophanes says that before he can say anything significant about Eros he must treat of the nature of man and the happenings (*pathémata*) that have befallen it; he must speak of the *destinies* of the soul (189 d). Sorry, but there is no simpler, quicker, and easier way to arrive at a knowledge of Eros, that most interesting of subjects.

What, then, is the nature of the soul—moreover, soul both "divine and human"? These last words seem to belie all that we normally associate with the concept of "soul." And indeed it soon becomes clear that Plato is not talking about what *we* mean by soul. *We*—that is to say those who, following the incorporation of Aristotle into European thought in the thirteenth century—understand "soul" to mean the principle of life which shapes the body from within, the *forma corporis*, which is to say, something that can exist only in the realm of physical beings. From that point of view, *divine soul* is a meaningless phrase. But we are not inclined to think that Plato uses meaningless language. What, then, does he mean? He means the quality common to both the human soul and to God: *spirituality*, which has the mode of being of *psyche*, of breath, *pneuma*. When we grandly talk about the "psychic," about "spirituality" or the "pneumatic" character of the mind, we are doing nothing but repeating variations of the word *breath*. What is meant, then, is the "breath of life," non-corporeal and vivifying at once. We must, says Socrates, ponder *this* aspect of the divine as well as the human mind; otherwise we shall not understand the nature of Eros or the gift which man is destined to receive when he is in love.

"Here then our pondering begins: All soul is immortal." To attempt to analyze the argument for the immortality of the soul would lead us too far afield. But since our normal habits of thinking would tend to make us misunderstand one point, that point must be discussed. It is the Platonic conception of immortality as extending not only into the future, but also into the past. Soul is not only imperishable, but also unborn, *agénetos*. Plato has nowhere expressed this idea so clearly as he does in the *Phaedrus*. We tend to regard this Platonic notion, which is rooted in the idea of the pre-existence of the soul, as beyond discussion, as something alien to us which we could not possibly endorse, something at any rate to be dismissed as incompatible with the Christian and Occidental conception of the human soul. But does not Christian doctrine at bottom agree with this Platonic idea? We too think of the spiritual soul as something that is not really "born." When we say that the soul is *immediately* "created," like all spiritual beings that enter into existence, are we not saying that the soul does not come to be in the same way that all other things grow and develop? There is no such thing as a genetics of the spiritual soul. This thesis—which, by the way, is of highly contemporary importance—is not merely similar to Plato's; it is exactly the same. I am not saying this in order to set up an artificial contemporary pertinence, but to make the present-day reader of Plato realize that such old and often-repeated doctrines are more than historically interesting. They seriously concern us, nowadays. Therein lies the greatness of Plato: that his insights cannot so easily be dismissed as no longer valid, even though the language in which he couches them may be questionable. They still concern us, and we find it by no means easy to substitute "better" insights for them.

This also applies to what is said about the soul in the following passages—as, for example, that it traverses the entire universe as if provided with wings. Kurt Hildebrandt [3] has rightly noted that here Plato returns to the views of pre-Socratic philosophy. This would seem to move the whole argument even further away from us, to realms of thought where we simply can no longer be expected to follow. How, for example, are we to be concerned with this fragment by Anaximenes the Milesian: "As the soul, which is air, permeates us, so also breath and air permeate the whose cosmos"? [4] And indeed, if by air was meant the meteorological phenomenon of the atmosphere, the dictum really would not concern us. But no one can ever persuade me that this ancient text does not also, and perhaps primarily, mean the same thing as the likewise ancient text about the spirit which fills the earthly sphere: *Spiritus Domini replevit orbem terrarum* (Wisdom 1, 7). That is, the abode of spirit is total reality. But from the most ancient times this has not been attributed to the divine Spirit alone; we cannot conceive and describe finite "spirit" save as a being whose nature it is to exist in the presence of total reality. This is what we mean by possession of spirit or soul: to be involved with *everything* that exists: "to permeate the whole cosmos."

Anyone who fails to consider this, Socrates says in the *Phaedrus*, does not understand what is truly happening in erotic emotion. The indubitably earthly, physical lover is shaken to his depths by the encounter with beauty, which is to say, once again with something earthly, physical, apparent to the senses. But in that overpowering emotion he is carried out of the dimension of the here and now, becomes unborn and imperishable, and his emotion cannot be satisfied with anything less than the Whole, the Totality of being, truth, goodness, beauty. The person who does not grasp this simply cannot understand what Love really is. He has absolutely no prospect of even finding the trail of erotic emotion, let alone tracing it to its source.

It might perhaps be argued that this is a "typically Platonic" idealization. But that is not so. It is a fully realistic description of what spirit really is.

Plato, to be sure, does not claim to be making a final and complete statement of what the nature of spirit is. Rather, he admits straightforwardly that he cannot do so. It would require *divine* speech to say what the "idea of soul" is: "Most assuredly a god alone could tell it." For in this case as in all others only he who knows the "idea," that is to say, the design of a reality, fully knows this reality; only he who knows the "idea" of a thing knows this thing as intensively as it can possibly be known at all; he alone "comprehends" the thing in the strict sense of the word (for "to comprehend" means to know something as intensively as it is possible to know it [5]). But such knowledge is not possible for the human mind. Only God, then, knows the nature of spirit. Nevertheless human language has a valuable function, as we read in the *Phaedrus*: man can say in figurative language what the soul resembles. And then follows the famous Platonic figure of the soul as a chariot team: "Let this [i.e., the human mode] be our manner of discourse. Let it, the soul, be likened to the union of powers in a team of winged steeds and their winged charioteer."

At this point we must interject a comment on Plato's style. Plato's philosophical language, as we know, is highly figurative. What relation, then, does his metaphorical speech bear to "truth"? How is it correlated to its subject? As soon as we examine his language from this point of view, it turns out that his figurativeness does not spring from a "poetic" carelessness toward exact rendition of reality, or from the reckless play of the creative imagination. Rather, Plato himself expressly terms it a kind of acquiescence in inadequacy, an expedient, a confession of failure. We are not able to speak of matters such as soul, spirit, deity, with any claim to direct description. This is Plato's excuse for attempting to explain the same thing by *several* analogies, as he is wont to do. The implication is that a matter is difficult or impossible to grasp by direct, non-metaphorical statement, and that no single metaphor is in itself completely adequate, none fully accurate.

At this point a second remark must be made that touches on basic principles. The figurative account, which comes next in the *Phaedrus* dialogue, on the nature and destiny of the human soul, is always called by Plato scholarship "the myth of the soul." [6] I should like to raise an objection here, chiefly to the loose usage of the term *myth*. In the strict sense, myth is a story dealing with the interplay between the divine and human spheres; it is not the invention of the narrator who happens to be telling it, but is rather something he is handing down from tradition. The recital of a genuine myth never begins as does the parable in *Phaedrus*. Instead, a myth is always ushered in with the words: *palai legetai*, "it has been said from olden times . . ."

This, of course, is only a side issue. What is crucial is the content of the parable. Perhaps we think we are already completely familiar with it: the charioteer who tries to control an unmatched team; one steed noble and docile, the other wild and refractory; the discordance between spirit and senses—and so on. It is already a little boring, we have heard it so often. We also think we understand it perfectly—only the exegesis does not happen to be accurate! There is not a word in this parable about the "discordance between spirit and the senses," not a word about what is generally considered to be Platonic doctrine: that the unhappiness of man springs from his physical being. The parable of the soul does not, to be precise, speak of man at all. The matter under discussion is the nature of the human mind. Plato is saying that the possibility of degeneration and downfall lies within the structure of the human mind itself, which is finite. Man is inclined toward and capable of wickedness not just because of physicality and sensuality. But because of what? Plato gives no explicit answer to this question, unless it is this: that the human mind, because it is non-divine, because it is finite, is susceptible to evil. The susceptibility is there *before* it encounters temptations from the sirens' song of the world of sense. "The will can be bent to evil; that is natural to it . . . by virtue of its origin from Nothingness." This sentence is not from Plato, but from Thomas Aquinas' *Quaestiones disputatae de veritate*.[7] Thus Thomas holds the same opinion as Plato (although, of course, he could never agree with what Plato goes on to say, that man himself actually came into being only as the result of a *fall* of the unmixed, pure soul). According to Plato, the soul of any tangible, physical man is a fallen pure spirit. This is equivalent to saying that the origin of physical man is the consequence of a fault—something that should not have happened. For elucidation of this thesis we are referred to "Orphic theology," which was the fountainhead for such notions; or else we are informed that the great early Christian theologian Origen explained the physicality of the entire world of substance as resulting from the fall of rebellious angelic spirits. All this sort of thing strikes us as infinitely remote from what we call "modern thought." Nevertheless we should remember that the history of thought constantly reverts to the fundamental ideas expressed by Plato in this parable. Those, for example, who know their Descartes [8] have pointed out that in all his statements about the human soul he assumes that the soul is a "pure angelic spirit" united with the body only by chance.

At any rate, Socrates goes on to say that everyone who claims to know something about Eros must take into account the accident that befell the soul in ancient times. The soul "permeates the whole world; but one that has shed its wings sinks down until it can fasten on something solid, and settling there it takes to itself an earthly body which seems by reason of the soul's power to move itself. This composite structure of soul and body is called a living being, and is further termed 'mortal.' " The metaphor may strike us as totally invalid; however, Plato has expressed an aspect of human existence which is difficult to describe in any other way. I am referring to the aspect of "yearning" and "recollection of origin." Both yearning and recollection of its origin are alien, indeed repellent, to the mind

246
c 2

that seeks to be autarchic and to dominate the world. Nevertheless we sense that we are profoundly right when we do not feel entirely at home in this world, in the here and now.

"Yearning" and "recollection" point back toward the original state of beginning, which concurrently appears as the true end and aim of life. We must pick out this one element from the complex tapestry of Plato's parable and keep our eyes fixed on it: the picture of the perfect life which was in the beginning and will be again in the end. The soul is a winged being. (Evidently we cannot put aside the notion of flying as liberation, any more than we can put aside the kindred notion that what is good for us is *above*; in dreams, particularly, these fancies seem virtually indestructible.) We do not have to underline the fact that Plato has nothing physiological or technical in mind when he speaks of the *winged* soul; what he means is that the soul has the power to ascend to the place of the gods. The power of ascent, however, is likewise strengthened by the nearness of the divine, which is beautiful and wise and good. The blessed life of the gods themselves is described as a passing to and fro in heaven, the gods' journeyings culminating in a great banquet. And the human soul participates in both the journeyings and the banquet. The feasting itself, however, the nourishment, the eating and drinking, take place in the form of contemplation. And what the soul contemplates—at the summit, standing "upon the back of the world"—is true Being, colorless, formless, intangibly real. And the soul delights in this; "contemplating truth she is nourished and prospers."

This, then, is what the soul which has fallen, through wickedness and forgetfulness, into the world of corporeal what is wrong; of ferment, unrest, helplessness. Among his images are some highly "unpoetic" ones; for example, Socrates speaks in the *Phaedrus* of the uncomfortable state of a teething child. Lovers—we may read this in Aristophanes' speech in the *Symposium*—do not know what they really want of one another; in fact it is evident that their two souls crave something else (something other than the pleasure of lovers' intercourse); but the soul cannot express what this other thing is, "of which she has only a dark and doubtful presentiment" (192 c–d).

At this point an important element emerges: the distinction between lust and love. The lustful know quite well what they want; at bottom they are calculating, see clearly, and "have their wits about them." But lust is not love; the object of desire is, strictly speaking, not loved; rather, that person is loved *for whom* something is desired. But the lover who thus loves without desire is not someone who is doing something of his own accord, or making something happen; rather, he "is moved" by the sight of his beloved. Now, says Plato, what is most beloved and most moving is beauty—for which reason those who love the fair are simply called "lovers" as a general denomination.

As latter-day, sophisticated readers of Plato we are continually tempted to regard such talk as sentimental, unrealistic romanticizing. But I think we would be wrong to do so. Plato is speaking quite soberly; he is not mistaken in suggesting that much, if not most, of what is ordinarily represented as love is nothing but lust. He knows that real ravishment by beauty is something rare. To be sure, Plato does insist that those rare cases must attain to the true aim of all encounters with beauty. "Few

82

men, remembers; and this is what it yearns for. N
soul is doomed to such forgetfulness and futile y
Here and there are those who keep themselves fr
special manner, and therefore have not lost their n
of an earlier blessed state. One can recover it all wh
"stands aside from the busy doings of mankind" an
forth out of the workaday world. But he who does
rebuked by the multitude as being out of his wits, for
know not that he is full of a god."

And now, at last, Socrates comes around to Love!
one form of this ecstatic *enthousiasmos* is the shock of e
tion caused by beauty, erotic *mania*. However, the sente
reveals its full significance only in its converse: l
reaches its apogee and attains its own potentialities only
awakening recollection, or rather, when it itself is rec
lection of something that exceeds any possibility of grati
cation in the finite realm.

The encounter with sensuous beauty gives rise to eroti
emotion. Beauty, earthly beauty, can strike the receptiv
mind more effectively, can hit home more powerfully, than
any other "value." It can prod man out of the realm of
comprehensible habituation, out of the "interpreted world"
in which (to invert Rilke's phrase [9]) he may have thought
himself very reliably at home. Everyday language bears
out the idea: we say that a thing of beauty is "ravishing."
And a person who is "ravished" has lost the calm security
of self-possession, if only for a moment; he is, we say,
"moved" by something else; he is passive. Plato repeatedly
finds new ways to describe this state, in which one is deprived of self-possession and shaken out of one's adjust-
ment to the world. He speaks of wanting to fly up and
being unable to; of being beside oneself and not knowing

indeed are left that can still remember . . . the holy objects of their vision."

But nothing evokes such memory so powerfully as beauty; that is one of its distinctive marks. In this power to point to something beyond the immediate present, beyond the world of here and now, beauty is comparable to nothing else in the world. Anyone who has grasped only a little of Plato's view of the world knows of his belief that everything we encounter in this world of experience, all reality, truth, good, is *image*—that is, it points to a prototype which is not directly encountered. We may possibly encounter the highest embodiment of goodness, justice, or wisdom—in the person of a just ruler, say—so that we cannot help feeling admiration and reverence. Nevertheless, such encounters do not have the power to shake us emotionally; they do not remove us from the here and now. Beauty alone can do that; only the encounter with beauty evokes remembrance and yearning, so that somebody deeply moved by beauty wishes to leave the orbit of ordinary human concerns.

Plato describes the distinctive mark of beauty on two levels: in the form of otherworldly experience (beauty in the heavens, once upon a time), and in the form of present existence (beauty in the here and now).

Apparently Plato envisages the utmost perfection accorded to man only as an encounter with divine Beauty, not as an encounter with the idea of Goodness or of Being —or anything else. If further proof of this were needed, we need only cite a few words from the speech of Diotima which Socrates reports in the *Symposium*—words, incidentally, that are likewise addressed directly to *Phaedrus* ("Such, Phaedrus and all of you, were the words of Diotima . . ."): "When he comes toward the end he will suddenly perceive a beauty of wondrous nature . . . not fair in the likeness of a face or hands or any other part of the bodily frame . . . but beauty absolute, separate, simple and everlasting. . . . Are you not certain that it will then be given to him to become a friend of God . . . ?" (211–212). And in the *Phaedrus* we read: "Once"—in Greek the word refers both to the past, primeval times, and to the future, the future of the end of time—"once when amidst that happy company, we beheld with our eyes that blessed vision, ourselves in the train of Zeus . . . then were we all initiated into that mystery which is rightly accounted blessed beyond all others. . . . Beauty shone bright amidst these visions."

On the level of ordinary existence, beauty is also something incomparably special. It is the most visible of all things; we perceive beauty through the clearest of our senses, the eye. *Pulchrum est quod visu placet*, beauty is what pleases the *beholder*. That is an unequivocal statement—neither a fragrance nor a taste nor an auditory impression can be "beautiful" in the strict sense. But nothing else in the spiritual realm presents itself so directly and visibly to our eyes. We cannot "see" wisdom, for example. If we could, Plato adds, if wisdom were to appear as clearly before our eyes as beauty, "how passionate had been our love for her"—a love shattering the frame of our life, ravishing us away out of our present existence. But for neither wisdom nor anything else worthy of love—"for beauty alone this has been ordained, to be most manifest to sense and most lovely of them all."

Once more let us stress that Plato is far from thinking that this effect is inevitable, that beauty always or even usually moves men so deeply. He is well aware that beauty can also arouse an impious, selfish lust. Only those who allow themselves to remember will experience the shock of emotion, the shudder of awe. Like a rain pouring in through the eyes, beauty makes the wings of the soul grow again, the wings which enable it to ascend to the abode of the gods, whence the soul has come. This, says Plato's Socrates, constitutes the true experience of love. The gods therefore call Eros not the Winged One, but the Giver of Wings—Plato at this point quotes an old verse to this effect.

251
b 1

252
b 4

It is the attribute of beauty, then, that it does not make us content, like something that "satisfies" us, even on the most spiritual level. We would not expect Goethe to espouse this idea—yet he does, and has summed up this Platonic concept in a single sentence of magnificent conciseness: "Beauty is not so much performance as promise." [10] That is, when we receive beauty in the proper way, we experience not so much a quenching of our thirst, satisfaction and pleasure, as evocation of an expectancy; we are referred to something that is not-already-present. Those who submit to the encounter with beauty in the requisite spirit do not see and partake of a fulfillment but a promise —which perhaps cannot be kept at all within the realm of this physical existence.

This last phrase is almost a quotation; it comes from a play by Paul Claudel. Woman, he says, is "the promise that cannot be kept; precisely in this does my grace consist." [11] Both Claudel and Goethe, it seems to me, are voicing the very sentiment expressed by Plato. For he tells us that the erotic emotion experienced in the encounter with beauty is a form of *theia mania,* of divine madness,

to the extent that what really takes place in it is not "gratification," not becoming at home in the here and now, but
rather opening the inner spaces of life to an infinite as-
suagement which cannot be had "here"—save in the form
of yearning and recollection. One who looks upon earthly
beauty and recalls true Beauty recovers his wings . . . ;
and so the true lover returns to the community of the gods
before the full term of banishment is over.

Now Plato goes on to assert that this is true not only for
the lover but also for the philosopher. We shall have to
pass rather rapidly over this initially perplexing association, which is also to be found in the *Symposium* (204).
But we must make clear that Plato here is scarcely indulg-
ing in an idle poetic fancy. On the contrary, he means
something quite precise. Lovers and men philosophizing
belong together to the extent that in erotic emotion and in
genuine philosophical inquiry something is activated which
cannot come to rest in the finite world. When a man encounters beauty which appeals to the senses, and is fully
receptive to that beauty, a passion is awakened which cannot be satisfied in the realm of sense—which is to say,
cannot be satisfied in what at first seems the only appropriate way. Similarly, in the very first stirrings of
philosophical astonishment (what does it mean, to be something real?) a question is raised which likewise cannot be
answered in the finite realm—which means in the way
"science," for example, would answer it. Both the philosopher and the true lover are insatiable—unless it happens
that they are accorded divine satiation.

Some of my readers, reviewing the essence of the discussion up to this point, may perhaps say that the conception is grand enough in all conscience, but also highly

"ideal," scarcely bearing upon the reality of actual men. Naturally it is difficult to argue with such an impression. Everything depends upon what we mean by human reality and real men. The crude reality of our starting point, the level of such categories as "success in love" or the "psychic hygiene of gratification of instincts" is certainly remote; that is clear. In the meantime we have almost forgotten this starting point, as, incidentally, we have almost forgotten that the discussion initially centered upon love for boys. But Plato would certainly not concede that the overwhelming emotion of the true lover is any less "real" than the lust which seeks immediate success, the direct gratification of the instincts.

Incidentally, Plato does not really set up a scheme or make "stipulations"; he merely describes a possibility. This is his thesis: in erotic emotion purely received and maintained, and perhaps in no other way, man can catch a glimpse of that promise which aims at a satiation affording deeper happiness than any gratification of the senses. Only in such a way, says Plato in the *Phaedrus*, can the profoundest meaning of Eros be achieved, that which Love really signifies.

But Plato can hardly be accused of withdrawing to a plane remote from life, as we see from the end of Socrates' speech. This conclusion is so amazing that a commentator like Wilamowitz is beside himself with astonishment. Why this, he says, is simply a contradiction of everything else that Plato has taught.[12]

Careful examination of the text shows that Socrates (Plato) speaks of four different forms or deformations of Love, which occur in human experience. The first one he mentions is the brutishness of the multitude, who want nothing but pleasure in the crudest sense of the word. No trace here of any romanticizing glossing of reality! Secondly, he speaks of the sophisticated sensuality of the proponents of rational techniques for living; the aim of these is, fundamentally, likewise nothing but pleasure. Thirdly, there is the love which renounces enjoyment; this is the most blissful form of love, the heroic achievement of love. He who loves in this manner leaves this earthly life "with burden shed and wings recovered" when he dies; he can forthwith ascend into the divine sphere and once more take part in the heavenly procession and in the Great Banquet of the gods.

256
b 3

But the surprise in all this lies in what Socrates has to say about the fourth form of love. (This, too, is where Wilamowitz is astonished.) Socrates speaks of the kind of love that is not wholly continent, but is still not simple lust; love that is true amorous passion, ravishment, devotion; non-calculating, powerful emotion. Such lovers will "carry off no mean reward for their lover's madness," for their *mania*, their self-forgetfulness, Socrates tells us. Their souls—in death—will leave the body not with perfect but with budding wings. Because they have already "taken the first steps on the celestial highway," they will no more return to the dark. Quite clearly, these words are intended eschatologically; Socrates is speaking of "salvation," and salvation is achieved only, though always, where true love exists. But those who possess only "worldly wisdom," who "dispensing a niggardly measure of worldly goods . . . engender in the soul an ignoble quality," will be plunged into darkness, into the opposite of salvation.

256
d 4

256
e 4

"Where else," Wilamowitz asks,[13] "has Plato shown such tolerance toward the weakness of the flesh?" It seems to me that this question does not strike at the heart of the matter. It is not that Plato is being lenient about the "sin of weakness." Rather, he is saying that this weakness can be outweighed, if not entirely reshaped and transformed, by the elevating power of true love. This is the decisive factor. "The worst disorders of the heart preserve a certain human grandeur and compel our respect if at their root there lies that passionate love which forgets everything else, above all the lover's own interests and own limits." [14] This must not be understood as a mere concession to human nature or to instinctuality. What Plato means is that love, insofar as it is real *ekstasis*, a stepping out of the narrow circle of the self-concerned ego, a frenzy, *mania*, is capable of carrying aloft with it even the heaviest burden, for it remembers the holy things it once contemplated.

254
b 5

VII

How does this accord with our own view of truth? Ultimate positions are staked. Real and apparent divergencies. Eros and agapé. The proximity of spirit and sensuality. Does unselfish love exist?

A great writer, especially when separated from us by long spans of time or cultural divergencies, often remains a mere historical phenomenon, a figure in a museum. He can become a vital intellectual force to the reader, someone whose doctrine or message can be really heard and put to use, only if the reader goes to the trouble of matching the writer's ideas against his own set of truths. When these ideas concern the meaning of the universe or the whole structure of human existence, the serious reader has to test these against his own convictions. He must be willing to stake his own position. In this sense, we can fruitfully study Plato's deepest statements about man only if we ourselves attempt to set the Platonic ideas against our own ultimate positions.

There is no reason to suppose that any such confrontation of Plato's ideas with our own notions of truth will yield only harmony and reciprocal confirmation. We must be prepared for the fact that profound disagreements may also come to light. But we should not be too hasty about defining those disagreements. Quite often we discover that even where we cannot fully accept Plato's literal statements, we find that they capture and express an aspect of reality which might otherwise have remained hidden from us.

Nevertheless, there are enough instances where our own viewpoint cannot easily—sometimes cannot possibly—be reconciled with Plato's. This is especially so in regard to the doctrine of Eros. Even if we leave aside the profound gulf which can be summed up by the word "pederasty," there remains, for example, the question of whether the kind of love which is first kindled by sensuous beauty is *the* basic form of love altogether. Is not what the Christian calls *caritas* and *agapé*, and which he considers love's highest manifestation, something altogether different, perhaps even non-erotic, that is to say, not only different from Eros but opposed to it? To be sure, would not such concepts be altogether beyond the scope of Plato, and pre-Christian man in general? Is it true that the powerful emotions aroused by beauty, even by obvious beauty that strikes directly at the senses, must always have an *erotic* character? Do we not have experiences with beauty (of a flower, say, or an architectural column, or of spiritual perfection embodied in something that appeals to the senses) which are totally non-erotic? Naturally, such questions take us far afield from our consideration of Plato, and this is no place to launch upon a thorough discussion of them, let alone to try to answer them.

First of all, we should remember that Plato, in taking the theme of Eros for his subject in the *Phaedrus*, is not presenting a systematic doctrine in the form of a continuous monologue. He intervenes in a conversation that has been going on for some time. A certain thesis has been proclaimed some time ago, apparently with great success (that is to say, persuasively enough to influence and shape the life of society). It is the thesis accepted and put into practice by the young intellectuals of contemporary Athens: that "love" has to do chiefly with pleasure and that the aim of life is to secure a maximum of such pleasure in an unsentimental and matter-of-fact manner, with a minimum of troublesome risks and complications. This thesis has been presented with a great display of sophisticated worldliness, but also with highly intelligent and even "moralistic" pseudo-arguments. Moreover, it represents the dominant view of sizable parts of society. Plato is therefore not beginning afresh at the bottom and constructing a comprehensive doctrine of human love. On the contrary, he is replying to an already existent doctrine; he is countering something, trying to correct what he regards as false views—although he is speaking from a viewpoint that embraces the whole of man's metaphysical position. He tries to show what love, initially sensual love which is kindled by physical beauty, is capable of becoming; what potentialities of richness and true possession of life can be thrown open and made accessible by love, perhaps only by love—if man himself does not corrupt love. But that is precisely the trouble, Plato says; for man is corrupting love when he pursues that seemingly so "reasonable" technique for living which aims at uncomplicated pleasure. In doing that he is practicing a form of self-betrayal which cheats him of his true potentialities.

Thus Plato's starting point is determined by what he is contending against. But he goes on to discuss the erotic emotion which is kindled by the encounter with sensuous beauty and to claim for it a significance capable of filling the entire space of the inner life.

Of course all kinds of doubts, questions, and objections can be raised here, too. We might, for example, wonder why what Plato considers to be the "energy of recollection" inherent in love, its power to give wings to the soul and lead the soul back to the abode of the gods, should have its seat so close to the realm of sense, of body, even of physiology. We might point out that in this very *Phaedrus* Plato clearly rejects the mingling, let alone identification, of love on the one hand and lust on the other. Incidentally, such a merging can proceed not only from "below," that is, from the "materialism" of mere desire for pleasure, but also from "above," from a "spiritualized" negation of the body and sensuality. From either point of view, love is declared to be a mere romantic masking of lust. Strangely enough, such a spiritualized negation of the body is always being called "Platonism," not only by those who are reckless with their labels, but also by such great Platonists as Plotinus. The biography of Plotinus written by his disciple Porphyrius began with the words: Plotinus was one of those who are ashamed to be in the body—an attitude, incidentally, which has always accompanied Christianity as a Manichaean undercurrent.

Although Plato, then, clearly rejects both the spiritualistic and the materialistic identifications of love and lust, he nevertheless insists on the adjacency of the two. He maintains that the erotic emotion, this same overpowering emotion which gives wings to the soul and leads it back home to the abode of the gods, has the character of *passio*, of ravishment by something in the visible world, and that therefore—like all other "passions"—it springs from the body and the senses. This Platonic idea is by no means incommensurate with classical Christian doctrine. For the latter has a clearly parallel view which holds that no intellectual and no spiritual love, neither the *dilectio* based upon voluntary choice nor the *caritas* based upon grace, can really be a living human act without *amor*.[1] But *amor* is *passio*; it is stirred by an actual encounter. This is not to say that intellectual and spiritual love is a mere "unfolding" of *amor*. Instead, Thomas Aquinas would undoubtedly say that *dilectio* and *caritas* can regulate, purify, and heal the *passio amoris*. It would seem that Thomas, like Plato, holds an opinion which a "Christian mind" infected by Manichaeism and spiritualism would find hard to accept: the opinion that *caritas* as a human act can neither be kindled nor kept alive if it is separated from the vital foundation of *passio amoris*. This thesis of the link between *amor* and *caritas*, or, in Platonic terms, of Eros being rooted in the sensual realm—the same Eros which seeks to carry us with the wings of birds to the abode of the gods—this thesis is far from being a mere theory of the nature of man. It is corroborated existentially in the experiences of treatment by depth psychology. For this modern branch of the art of healing demonstrates that any harsh repression of the capacity for erotic emotion which is rooted in the realm of the senses makes love altogether impossible. Both intellectual and spiritual love are smothered. It shows, further, that the intolerance, harshness, and rigidity frequently found in men who seek to lead a "spiritual" life may well be caused by unnatural repression of the *passio amoris*.[2] Man is a physical being, even to the point of sublimest spirituality. But his physicality, which compels him to be a man or a woman even in the most spiritual expression of vitality, is not necessarily only a barrier and limitation. It is simultaneously the overflowing vital source of all human activity. Thomas Aquinas and Plato agree on that point.

Still another much-discussed divergence between the Platonic conception of love and our own doctrine proves, on closer examination, to be inconsequential. Plato's concept of Eros, it is said, refers, basically, to self-love, to egotistic seeking for enrichment and fulfillment, whereas the Christian concept of *caritas-agapé*, on the contrary, is of a renunciatory, unselfish, giving love. To contrast the two kinds of love in this manner is a dreadful simplification. Moreover, we may well take issue with the way they have been described. Thus, Plato also holds that the love which has ascended to behold the source of beauty is so transformed that it leaves all selfish volition far behind it; it can best be described as "adoration." Certainly this emerges from the conclusion of Diotima's reported speech in the *Symposium* (211–212). In the second place, it is extremely questionable whether man is at all capable of loving in a completely "unselfish" way. Even in Christian theology, the highest form of *caritas* is defined as loving God as the *dispenser of bliss*.[3] But bliss, which is ultimately sought in all love, is nothing but the final quenching of the deepest thirst. Man is by nature a thirsting and needy being—not only, as Kant said, insofar as he "belongs to the world of sense," [4] but also and especially insofar as he is spirit. It is not in our power to be so "unselfish" that we can renounce the ultimate quenching of our thirst, bliss. We *cannot* want not to be blissful.[5]

VIII

*The second part of the dialogue.   What makes a speech "beautiful"?
Does truth also have need of rhetoric?   The great teachers do not
write.   Prayer for "beauty within."*

In the "recantation," the real speech on love which forms
the heart of the *Phaedrus*, Socrates spoke with a wholly
pure, unironic emotional force rare in the Platonic dialogues. He actually apologizes for this tone, though he
does this quite ironically, in the final petition which is
directly addressed to Eros the god: "I have offered the
fairest recantation and fullest atonement that my powers
could compass; some of its language, in particular, was
perforce poetical, to please Phaedrus." We then have something that is a regular procedure in the Platonic dialogues:
everything imaginable is done to destroy any "solemnity"
that may have arisen. At one blow the whole atmosphere is
again changed, and there follows a playful sprinkling of
what seem random inspirations chosen on a purely associa-
tive basis. Socrates himself calls it a game: "Then we may
regard our literary pastime as having reached a satisfactory
conclusion. . . ." This second part of the dialogue, which is
full of witty allusions to celebrities of contemporary Athens,
probably seemed extremely lively to the readers of Plato's

237
a 5

278
b 7

time. For us, however, the full force of its topical references is lost.

On the other hand, it would be strange if this part of the dialogue did not also relate to its basic theme. For example, it is all part and parcel of the total situation which the dialogue treats that, for Lysias and his public, content is entirely subsidiary to the matter of style. The whole discussion of Eros, that is, sprang from a speech which was considered purely as rhetoric, publicity writing, literature. Its purpose was to impress and dazzle. It was also to be adaptable to another's use, for therein lay its chances for achieving its purpose (and this, in turn, is not unrelated to content). Thus it is no accident that the casual noonday conversation under the plane tree turns to the old Socratic subject: what really makes a speech *beautiful*; whether one really has to know what one is talking about; and whether it is not important to speak the truth. Let us recall how Socrates, in an earlier dialogue, summed up what the Sophist Gorgias had to say about his own art: "The nature of rhetoric is this: it need not be familiar with the subjects themselves, nor need it know what their state is; it must only possess a technique of persuasion which awakens in the ignorant the conviction that the speaker is more knowing than the knowledgeable" (459 b–c). Phaedrus gives almost exactly the same answer, obviously one

260
a 4

learned in school: so far as he knows, the successful orator need only know what people *think* is the truth; rhetoric is based on persuasion and not on truth. Thereupon Socrates, with the infinite patience of the educator, begins right at the beginning again, and in his usual fashion with a highly

260
b 1

specific example: "Suppose I tried to persuade you to acquire a horse for use in battle against the enemy, and suppose that neither of us knew what a horse was, but I knew this much about you, that Phaedrus believes a horse to be that tame animal which possesses the largest ears.—A ridiculous thing to suppose, Socrates.—Wait a moment: suppose I continued to urge upon you, in all seriousness, with a studied encomium of a donkey, that it was what I called it, a horse. . . ." And so on. The important part of this is the conclusion: If the matter at issue were not horse and donkey, but good and evil, "what kind of crop do you think such oratory is likely to reap from the seed thus sown?"

And then, abruptly, the discussion turns to an utterly different question. Probably it was one that troubled Plato all his life. Friedländer [1] quotes the penetrating epigram of Novalis, "Polemic is struggle against the self," and wonders whether Plato, in all these masterfully imitated Sophistic speeches in his dialogues, "did not also have, as a possible danger, something of the versatility of his Sophists." And indeed we must not let ourselves forget what enormous inner tension must have been present in Plato's voluntary attachment to Socrates. Throwing the tragedies into the fire—that was a swift, heroic act. But what enabled him and impelled him to write those tragedies could surely not be cast aside so easily. We must recall this in order to perceive the special meaning of the question which Plato puts into the mouth of Socrates himself in the *Phaedrus*: *whether truth also may not have need of rhetoric*. Socrates, for his part, gives the "perhaps too scurrilously abused" art of rhetoric a chance to speak in its own defense: "Without my aid even the real knower of truth will not be able to persuade anybody!" It almost seems as if Plato cannot talk about this subject with complete

260
d 5

impartiality. On the one hand he is by nature a great writer extremely sensitive to the nuances of language. He himself would know how to manipulate all the arts of the Sophists with sovereign ease. On the other hand he nevertheless continues to feel the spell of Socrates, whose life runs counter to all formal culture, who speaks in a wholly un-literary manner, and who aggressively and ironically re-pudiates anything which goes beyond speaking the bare truth. A generation later, Plato's pupil Aristotle, untouched by this conflict, will write a philosophical book on rhetoric with utter lack of embarrassment. All the same, Aristotle too upheld what Socrates in the *Phaedrus* calls the heart of all true rhetoric: to know the subject and to present its truth to listeners and readers so that the truth is apparent. The lecture Socrates gives young Phaedrus sounds almost like an enjoinder directed to Plato himself: a man whose example I would pray that we might follow, Phaedrus, will regard as his legitimate children only speeches on justice, beauty, and goodness which are expounded solely *for the sake of truth*. With these words, the merely tech-nical preoccupation with Maxims and Imageries, Brevi-ties, Prolixities, Pathetic Passages, Calumny and Refuta-tion of Calumnies—all that is swept from the table as so much claptrap.

But suddenly this noonday chat, which is apparently taking its own random course, once more moves toward a completely different subject, which nevertheless is highly pertinent. Phaedrus has brought Lysias' speech with him in the form of a scroll. That is to say, we are dealing with the written word, with "literature." Something inevitable and at the same time profoundly ambiguous has been set afoot. And Plato himself has personally experienced both the inevitability and the ambiguity—so that this great writer now writes about the perilousness of writing. Socrates tells Phaedrus the story of the invention of the alphabet. When Tammuz sat upon the throne of Egypt, there came to him Thoth, the inventor, who praised alphabetic writing as a "medicine for memory and wisdom." Thereupon the wise king replied that writing would have just the opposite effect. "If men learn this, it will implant forgetfulness in their souls; they will . . . rely on that which is written, calling things to remembrance no longer from within themselves, but by means of external marks."

274
c 5

This story belongs among the great statements of human wisdom, and should never be allowed to fade from the memory of man. It makes the eternally modern point that technical improvements which to all appearances facilitate man's participation in reality and truth actually do just the opposite: they hamper and possibly even destroy that participation. The ease of communication abolishes real communication. Once again we may say that Plato could not help coming to this conclusion as a result of his association with Socrates and his lifelong meditation upon the man. The very great teachers do not write. Few will guess that this last sentence is an almost literal quotation from the *Summa theologica* of Thomas Aquinas,[2] who specifically mentions Socrates in connection with this statement. Thomas asks whether Christ should not have set down his doctrine in writing—and answers that the higher mode of teaching is proper to the greater teacher, and that that higher mode consists in impressing his doctrine upon the hearts of his hearers. "Thus among the pagans Socrates and Pythagoras, who were the greatest teachers, *excellentissimi doctores*, did not wish to write anything down." Perhaps this thought throws a little light on the curious fact that Plato, throughout his at least fifty years as a writer, wrote nothing but dialogues. In dialogue alone, as Plato declared in his old age—in his seventh letter (341 d)—the spark of truth leaps abruptly into the soul. Of course Plato's works are nevertheless *written* dialogues, "literature." But "the dialogue is the only form of book which seems to suspend the book form itself." ³ And there is also the mysterious dictum of the seventy-five-year-old Plato in this same letter, that he has written nothing and will write nothing concerning "what really matters"; that the written word, insofar as the writer is a man, is never truly serious; "seriousness stays in the fairest abode of his thoughts" (344 c). This late, enigmatic statement is probably also connected with the story of the invention of the alphabet which Socrates tells to young Phaedrus in the noonday shade of the plane tree by the Ilissus.

Quite a few other matters are tossed back and forth in conversation. And there are a good many sentences that

272
c 10

270
c 1

278
d 3

startle the reader—for example: "Practice justice and advocate even the rights of the wolf"; or: "Do you think it possible to understand the nature of the soul satisfactorily without understanding the nature of the universe?" Here, too, we may find the pregnant distinction between human *philosophia* and the wisdom (*sophia*) which can be ascribed only to God.

Finally, the key word of the great speech on Eros returns once more: *beauty*. Behind all the ironic banter with which old Socrates, ugly as Silenus, habitually makes fun of himself, there sounds the note of deep seriousness, which it is impossible to misconstrue. Phaedrus jumps up and wants to return home to the city: "But let us be going, now that it has become less oppressively hot." Socrates, however, asks whether he does not think it fitting to offer a prayer. And then he makes his prayer to "Pan and all the other gods." It begins with the words:

"Grant that I may become fair within, and that such outward things as I have may not war against the spirit within me."

Notes

FOREWORD

[1] Fr. Überwegs, *Grundriss der Geschichte der Philosophie*, I (Berlin, 1926), p. 283.
[2] *Platons Phaidros* (Kiel, 1953), p. 15.
[3] Z. Diesendruck, *Struktur und Charakter des platonischen Phaidros* (Vienna, Leipzig, 1927), p. 2.
[4] *Platons Werke*, I (Berlin, 1804), p. 46.
[5] *Die genetische Entwicklung der platonischen Philosophie* (Leipzig, 1855), I, p. 275.
[6] *Philologus*, 48 (1898), pp. 428 f.
[7] *Platon. Sein Leben und seine Werke* (Berlin, Frankfurt a. Main, 1948), p. 361.
[8] *Platons Phaidros*, p. 69.
[9] *Die Abfassungszeit des platonischen Phaidros*, Rheinisches Museum (1880), pp. 131 f.
[10] Cf. Diesendruck, p. 6.
[11] Ibid., p. 33.
[12] P. 374.

I

[1] *Platon*, p. 374.
[2] Ibid.
[3] Pauly-Wissowa, *Real-Enzyklopädie der klassischen Altertumswissenschaft*, art. "Phaidros," col. 1556 f.
[4] Ibid., art. "Lysias," col. 2535.
[5] Ibid., art. "Epikrates," col. 119.
[6] Ibid., art. "Morychos," col. 326.

[7] *Paideia*, I (New York, 1945), p. 313.

[8] *Lectures on the History of Philosophy* (transl. E. S. Haldane, London, 1892), I, p. 371. [*Sämtliche Werke (Jubiläumsausgabe)*, ed. H. Glockner, Vol. 18 (Stuttgart, 1928), p. 27.]

[9] *Plato's Theory of Man* (Cambridge, Mass., 1948), p. 283.

[10] *The Philosophy of History* (transl. J. Sibree, Dover Publications, New York, 1956), p. 269. [*Vorlesungen über die Philosophie der Weltgeschichte*, ed. G. Lasson (Leipzig, 1923), III, p. 643.]

[11] *Discourse on Method*, chap. 6.

[12] If, however, the clear meaning of the Greek text (*eron* is the participle of *erao*, I love) is misconstrued (as it is by K. Hildebrandt and L. Georgii) and translated not as "lover" and "non-lover," but as "the infatuated" and "the non-infatuated," the seriousness and the real meaning of Plato's argument are distorted beyond recognition.

II

[1] Reinhold Schneider, *Winter in Wien* (Freiburg i. Br., 1958), p. 153.

[2] K. Hildebrandt, *Platons Phaidros*, p. 37.

[3] P. Friedländer, *Platon*, III (Berlin, 1960), p. 203. Friedländer quotes J. Vählen (*Über die Rede des Lysias in Platons Phaidros*. Sitzungsberichte der Berliner Akademie, 1903).

[4] R. Hackforth, *Plato's Phaedrus. Translated with Introduction and Commentary* (Cambridge, England, 1952), p. 17, note 4.

[5] *Platons Phaidros*, p. 38.

[6] *Platon*, III, p. 203.

[7] Hackforth, p. 27.

[8] A. E. Taylor quoted in Hackforth, p. 31.

[9] Cf. Thomas Aquinas, *Quaestiones disputatae de veritate*, 26, 7 ad 1.

[10] Book I, chap. 14.

[11] *Platons Phaidros*, p. 38.

III

[1] Cf. Hackforth, p. 34, note 1.

[2] *Platons sokratische Periode und der "Phaidros."* Philosophische Abhandlungen für Max Heinze (1906), p. 787. Cf. Diesendruck, p. 13.

3 Cf. J. Pieper, *Leisure the Basis of Culture* (New York, 1964), pp. 15 f.

4 H. Gauss in his interpretation of *Phaedrus* (*Philosophischer Hand-kommentar zu den Dialogen Platons*, Bern, 1958) takes Socrates' first speech as an attempt "first of all to put the ideas of Lysias in logical order" (p. 243). It seems to me that this misses the crucial point.

5 *Platon*, III, p. 207.

6 Cf. R. Guardini, *The Death of Socrates* (Meridian Books, New York, 1962), pp. 49 f.

IV

1 "On My Work as Author," in *The Point of View* (transl. Walter Lowrie, Oxford, 1939), pp. 148 f.

2 "The Point of View for My Work as an Author," op. cit., p. 26.

3 *Platon*, p. 362.

4 Euripides, *Iphigenia in Tauris*, 1193.

5 "A Greek would have said [of repentance]: Thus slaves may feel!" *Fröhliche Wissenschaft* [*The Joyful Wisdom*], Book 3, No. 135.

6 *Politics*, 8, 6 (1341 a).

V

1 Pierre Amandry, *La mantique Apollonienne à Delphes* (Paris, 1950), pp. 43 f.

2 *Platon*, p. 361.

3 *Sibyllinische Weissagungen*, ed. A. Kurfess (Munich, 1951), p. 16.

4 Fragment 92 (Diels).

5 C. S. Lewis, *The Screwtape Letters* (New York, 1943), pp. 139 f.

6 *Aeneid*, 6, 42 ff. (*Virgil*, transl. H. R. Fairclough, Loeb Classical Library, Cambridge, Mass., 1935, Vol. I, pp. 509 ff.).

7 *Aeneid*, 6, 100 f.

8 *Aeneid*, 6, 11 f.

9 *Ver.* 13, 1 obj. 1.

10 *Summa theologica*, II, II, 171, 2.

11 *Ver.*, 12, 1.

12 *Ver.*, 12, 1 ad 1.

13 *Sum. theol.*, II, II, 171 prolog.

14 *Ver.*, 12, 2 ad 1.

[15] Friedländer, *Platon*, III, p. 210.
[16] *Platon*, p. 375, note 1.
[17] Ibid., p. 322, note 3.
[18] P. 60.
[19] Cf. *Reallexikon für Antike und Christentum*, I, col. 795.
[20] Quoted in Jolande Jacobi, *The Psychology of C. G. Jung*, 6th ed., rev. (London, New Haven, 1962), p. 72. [*Die Psychologie von C. G. Jung* (Zurich, 1940), p. 87.]
[21] *The Practice of Psychotherapy*, The Collected Works of C. G. Jung, 16 (New York, London, 1954), p. 59. [*Seelenprobleme der Gegenwart* (Zurich, 1951), p. 11.]
[22] Ibid.
[23] A. Görres, *Methode und Erfahrungen der Psychoanalyse* (Munich, 1958), p. 274.
[24] *Epistolae*, 115, 18.
[25] *Platon*, p. 376.
[26] Christiane Osann, *Rainer Maria Rilke* (Zurich, Leipzig, 1941), p. 7.
[27] *Soll die Dichtung das Leben bessern?* (Wiesbaden, 1956), p. 27.
[28] *Hamburgische Dramaturgie* (sections 101–104), April 19, 1768.
[29] Preface to *Bunte Steine*.
[30] To F. W. Riemer (1803–1813, Insel-Verlag, 1921), p. 334.
[31] To Chr. G. D. Nees von Esenbeck on July 23, 1820.
[32] To W. v. Rumohr on September 28, 1807.
[33] G. Benn, "Probleme der Lyrik," in *Essays, Reden, Vorträge* (Wiesbaden, 1959), p. 495.
[34] *Soll die Dichtung das Leben bessern?*, pp. 20, 16.
[35] Wiesbaden, 1957, p. 327.
[36] *Die Neue Rundschau*, No. 68 (1957).
[37] Ibid., p. 453.
[38] Ibid., p. 455.
[39] Ibid., p. 456.

VI

[1] Part I, Book 5.
[2] André Gide, *Journal 1889–1939* (Paris, Gallimard, 1948), Vol. II. [English version, translated by Justin O'Brien (New York, Knopf, 1951), II, 288.]
[3] *Platons Phaidros*, p. 47.
[4] Fragment 2 (Diels).

5 Thomas Aquinas, *Commentary on the Gospel of John*, 1, 11.
6 Cf. particularly K. Hildebrandt, *Platons Phaidros*, p. 57.
7 *Ver.* 22, 6 ad 3.
8 J. Maritain, *Trois Réformateurs* (Paris, 1925), pp. 75 ff.
9 First Duino Elegy.
10 *Campagne in Frankreich*, section entitled "Münster," December, 1792.
11 P. Claudel, *The City*, end of Third Act.
12 *Platon*, p. 369.
13 Ibid.
14 Ch. Couturier, *Discours de mariage*, Paris.

VII

1 Cf. Thomas Aquinas, *Sum. theol.*, I, II, 26, 3.
2 Cf. *Anima*, 1957, No. 3 (Sonderheft), p. 236.
3 Thomas Aquinas, *Sum. theol.*, II, II, 23, 1.
4 *Critique of Practical Reason*, Part I, Book I, 2nd Principal Part, p. 80. [*Kritik der praktischen Vernunft*, ed. by K. Vorländer (Leipzig, 1920).]
5 Thomas Aquinas, *Summa contra Gentiles*, 4, 92; *Sum. theol.*, I, II, 13, 6.

VIII

1 *Platon*, I, p. 178.
2 *Sum. theol.*, III, 42, 4.
3 Friedländer, *Platon*, I, p. 177.